Organ Cases of Western Europe

Michael I. Wilson

ORGAN CASES OF WESTERN EUROPE

C. Hurst and Company, London

First published in the United Kingdom by
C. Hurst & Co. (Publishers) Ltd,
1–2 Henrietta Street, London WC2E 8PS

PHOTOGRAPHY BY AD WINDIG

ISBN 0-903983-89-3

Designed by Alan Bartram
Produced for the publishers by
Lund Humphries Publishers, London
Plates printed in The Netherlands by
Nederlandse Rotogravure Maatschappij, Leiden
Text printed and bound in Great Britain by
W & J Mackay Ltd, Chatham, Kent

Contents

7 Foreword

9 Introduction
9 *Types of Organ*
9 *General Principles of Design*
15 *Styles of Decoration*
16 *Siting*
18 *The Makers*

19 Captions to the Plates
21 *Netherlands (North)*
33 *Netherlands (South)*
39 *Austria, Germany, Switzerland*
49 *Denmark*
52 *France*
61 *Spain, Portugal*
68 *Italy*
75 *British Isles*

81 Plates

361 List of Plates

367 Lists of the various artists and craftsmen mentioned in this book
367 *Organ builders*
368 *Architects*
368 *Painters*
369 *Woodcarvers, sculptors and cabinet-makers*

371 Bibliography

Foreword

This book is the fruit of a project originally envisaged a decade or more ago by the Dutch publisher Lucas Bunge. Since that time its scope and format have been changed more than once, and a number of recognised authorities have made invaluable contributions to the background knowledge from which it has been built up. Amongst these the author and publisher are especially indebted to the following: A. B. Correa, G. A. C. de Graaff, J. J. van der Harst, Lady Jeans, G. Lhôte, Dr G. Persoons, Gh. Potvlieghe, Dr D. Shanks, W. Shewring, the late Dr W. L. Sumner, Dr W. Supper, Professor L. F. Tagliavini, A. Verbene and Finn Viderø.

This is not, however, a book for the organ specialist. It is intended primarily for all those interested in the design and appearance of organ cases, be they organ builders or architects, organists or artists, clergy or laity, professionals or amateurs—or simply those who are drawn to visual beauty for its own sake. This being so, there will be found very little reference to technical data or to the organs themselves as musical instruments, especially since on the whole few extant old cases contain much more than the mere vestiges, if that, of the instruments they were originally designed to house. Thus, although in most instances the name of the original builder is given, the reader may safely assume that his instrument has long since been rebuilt and/or restored out of all recognition. A clear distinction must at all times be made between the case and its contents, for their several dates of construction may be separated by very many years. Most of the cases shown are of the seventeenth and eighteenth centuries.

Nor, of course, have the cases themselves escaped alteration, as the reader will soon discover. Some were never especially beautiful, and indeed it is not the primary purpose of this book to present only the finest organ cases in Europe, but rather a general critical review in which the selection ranges deliberately from the excellent to the ill-conceived and even ugly. At the same time the author's aesthetic judgements are his own and he does not expect his readers necessarily to agree with him.

The plates and relevant text are arranged under their appropriate European countries. For this purpose the Netherlands have been divided into North and South, the latter approximating to the area known today as Belgium, the former to the present-day Netherlands.

The names of towns and villages, and of the cathedrals and churches in them, are given in the vernacular of the country in which they are situated. This, it is hoped, may enable the 'organ-crawling' tourist to locate them more easily in his guidebook or on the map.

In discussing the plans of organ case-fronts, rounded towers are symbolised by 'u', pointed ones by 'v', the intervening flats by a line, thus – . Hence e.g. the arrangement u–v–u–v–u indicates a front consisting of three rounded towers and two pointed ones divided by four flats. (The terms 'rounded' and 'pointed' as applied to towers of course refers throughout to their form on plan, not in elevation.)

Introduction

Types of Organ

The basic parts of an organ are (a) a musical scale of whistle-type pipes; (b) a wind supply; (c) a keyboard and mechanism for conveying wind to pipes. When faced with a large instrument such as that in Chartres cathedral (126) or the St Bavo church in Haarlem (29), this statement may seem to be a dangerous simplification. Yet the fact remains that a large pipe organ is merely a highly sophisticated development of the same basic essentials.

Although known to the Romans, the organ had to be re-discovered by Western Christendom, where by the early Middle Ages it had become accepted as a regular adjunct to religious worship and secular merrymaking. By *c.* 1250 it had evolved into three separate types, each with a different usage, i.e.:

1. The portative organ. This was the basic instrument as outlined above, consisting of a simple scale of small pipes, standing on a box (the wind-chest), to the opposite sides of which were attached a miniature keyboard (little more than an octave in compass) and a correspondingly small pair of bellows. A strap suspended the organ round the neck of the player, who pumped the bellows with one hand whilst playing on the keyboard with the other. Owing to its convenient portability (hence its name) the instrument was used in processions and on similar occasions. Despite its small size it was nevertheless highly esteemed, and at least one virtuoso organist, the blind Italian Francesco Landini (1325–97), made his name on it rather than on the organ proper, although he was the official organist of San Lorenzo in Florence.

2. The positive organ. This was larger and heavier than the portative, and had to be set down for playing (Latin derivation: *ponere, posui, positum*—to set down or place), though it could be transported from one site to another. It required the services of one or more assistants to pump the bellows as well as those of the organist himself. Both portative and positive could be, and were, used for secular as well as religious music, and were as much at home in palaces, castles and houses as in churches or cathedrals.

3. The large, immobile church organ proper. The sounds produced by its pipes were unsubtle, while the mechanism of its crude keyboard was so heavy, resistant and indeed physically tiring that at suitable opportunities during services the organist would turn aside with relief to the lighter and more rewarding positive organ which often seems to have been placed near at hand for this purpose.

General Principles of Design

The idea of placing an organ within a housing or case probably first originated with the positive and was only later applied to the large organ. The pipes of an organ vary in length according to their pitch; the deeper the note the longer the pipe, the higher the note the shorter the pipe. Thus in the simplest form of organ the pipes (placed immediately over the keyboard) decrease in size as the notes get higher, their tops following a curve that is not regular but flattens out somewhat as the upper part of the compass is approached.

The visual effect of this curve is unaesthetic in all but the very smallest organs such as the portatives. At some time, therefore, it must have occurred to an organ builder that if the pipes of a positive organ were to be contained within a form of decorative cupboard the instrument's appearance would be greatly enhanced, especially if the cupboard were to be carved, painted or otherwise suitably embellished. Doors could entirely conceal the pipes when the instrument was not in use, keep dust and dirt from pipes and mechanism, and complete the illusion of a piece of furniture, whether domestic or ecclesiastical.

It is not possible to say when this development took place. However, it was probably an established fact by the mid-fourteenth century, even though both the positives in the famous paintings by Hugo van der Goes (*The Trinity Altarpiece*, *c.* 1478, on loan from H.M. the Queen to the National Gallery of Scotland, Edinburgh) and Jan van Eyck (*The Adoration of the Lamb*, 1432, St Bavon cathedral, Ghent) are unenclosed. (It is interesting to note that in the van der Goes painting two of the bass pipes—perhaps drones—are accommodated in a little castellated tower of their own, attached to the end of the main case.) Some positives, like the one in Hans Burgkmair's great series of engravings *The Triumphs of Maximilian*, had detachable covers.

Nor can it be said with certainty when the idea of a case was first applied to the large Gothic organ. The principle is already clearly established in the ancient case at Salamanca (141) which dates from the fourteenth century. This suggests little of the glories that were to come before long, and has a severely practical aspect. The clergy, however, cannot long have remained oblivious to the possibilities of using the organ case as a ground for paintings, a vehicle for conveying the Church's teachings pictorially to the faithful, just as they made use of stained glass and wall paintings. Hence the development during the Gothic period of the case with wings, painted on both sides, the whole design so reminiscent of an altar triptych that some authorities have raised the question as to which may have come first, organ case or triptych. Moreover, both have acoustical properties, in that in an organ case the wings helped to project the sound of the instrument, whilst in a triptych they gave the same assistance to the priest's voice. (In Spain there is an obvious connection between the design of organ cases and that of the great painted many-tiered altarpieces to be found in so many of the churches and cathedrals there.)

Whatever their origins, painted wings soon became an important feature of organ cases, especially in Germany, the Netherlands and, to a lesser extent, Italy. As their importance grew, artists of increasingly higher calibre were invited to decorate them. The ever-growing complexity of front plans meant that the simple flat wings soon evolved into complicated hinged shutters, and for these it was often found more convenient to use canvas stretched on wooden frames rather than solid wooden planks.

It soon became apparent that a case could benefit the large organ additionally by protecting it in some measure not only from dust but also from vermin (especially noted for chewing the bellows leather), birds (which got in via the church doors and as yet unglazed windows), vandals, and changes in temperature (though medieval man did not of course recognise this last hazard for what it was). Furthermore the case acts as a resonator; a fairly wide and shallow one produces a better acoustical result than one which is tall and deep. This being so, many Gothic cases must have encouraged a better tone than that produced from some of the organs housed later in the more elaborate cases of the Renaissance and Baroque eras.

Few if any of the remaining late Gothic cases of North Europe are still in their original state. Yet enough has survived for certain basic principles common to their design to be cited.

First, keyboard mechanism, though growing more complex, had become much lighter and more manageable, and by 1400 the roller board had been invented. The purpose of the keyboard mechanism is ultimately to admit air via the wind-chest to the pipe or pipes which correspond to the note being played. In the early organs such pipes were necessarily placed on the wind-chest immediately above the keys which served to operate them, but the roller board is a system of extended lever mechanism which makes it possible for the action to be transmitted laterally and, if necessary, for some distance from key to pipe. Thanks therefore to this invention pipes no longer had to stand in strict chromatic order but could be disposed within the case front in visually balanced groups. (This result is also achieved by leading the wind to the pipes in tubes rather than forcing them to stand immediately on the wind-chest.) Thanks also to the same invention the upper section or superstructure of the case containing the pipes could now be allowed to overhang the lower section or substructure (containing the keyboard and wind-supply mechanisms) at each end, making for a far more graceful and less box-like shape for the case. (The dividing line between the upper and lower case sections is conveniently, though inaccurately, given the architectural term 'impost'.)

Secondly, the principle of stop mechanism had been introduced. The medieval church organ had, it seems, several pipes to each key on the manual. Only one pipe produced the basic note appropriate to its key; the others produced fifths and octaves of that note, all, however, sounding together. This massed sound was continued throughout the instrument's entire compass in the different ranks of pipes, and is given the descriptive German term *Blockwerk*. Only in Italy was there any attempt from the start to isolate the parallel ranks of pipes from each other. However, it was eventually also established in North Europe that a mechanism could be used to admit air to selected ranks of pipes only, and thus was born the idea of 'stops', separate ranks of differently-constructed pipes which produced different types of tone-colour and were activated by knobs (drawstops) or levers beside the keyboard.

This idea, like that of the case itself, was probably first applied to the positive organ. Just as the use of the positive was a physical relief from the playing of the large organ, so its individual stops made for welcome aural contrast with the solid, unvarying sound of the *Blockwerk*. For convenience the positive was placed close beside the organist or even sometimes immediately behind him, so that he had to turn completely round from the keyboard of the main organ in order to play that of the positive. The final integration of the positive within the general design of the organ case is one of the features of late Gothic and Renaissance church-organ building, although in a secular context as opposed to a religious one the positive retained its separate identity and became known as the chamber or house organ.

The large classical organ is generally agreed to have first achieved a high level of development, both tonal and visual, in the northern areas of Germany and in the Netherlands by the early sixteenth century. Here too was born the idea that the instrument's tonal structure should be reflected in its appearance. In the earlier Gothic cases the pipes of the main organ stood in a straight row along the impost, their mouths at the same level right across the front of the organ (since the V-shaped feet were at that time all made exactly the same length). In the developed instrument of North Europe the pipes were disposed in a series of towers and flats (compartments whose front edge is straight, on plan) whose appearance and arrangement became increasingly complex as time wore on. As will shortly be explained, the arrangement of the pipes themselves became an essential feature of the overall design.

Below the main case was the positive, now firmly and permanently sited behind the player's back and usually appended to the organ gallery, established as an integral part of the main instrument and in its appearance often a more or less faithful miniature reflection of the main case. Keyboard action was transmitted to it from the main organ by lever systems running beneath the gallery floor, but in a number of organs the actual drawstops continued to be situated in the positive case itself, the organist still having to turn round in order to change them. In some instances the organist's bench was incorporated into the back of the positive case.

Each European country developed its own terminology for the different sections of the large organ, but then as now the most comprehensive descriptions were those in German and, to a lesser extent, Dutch. This is not surprising, since it was in Germany and the Netherlands that the development of the organ was at its most advanced. The German term for the main organ was *Hauptwerk*, for the positive *Rückpositiv* (lit. 'back positive', because of its position). In practice this term is often shortened to *Positiv*, the form which has been adopted in this book (the equivalent terms in other languages are also given under their appropriate countries). As time went on and the instruments grew larger, additional sections named *Oberwerk* (placed over the *Hauptwerk*) and *Brustwerk* (placed below the *Hauptwerk* and immediately over the keyboards) were added. Occasionally the entire composition was topped by a *Kronwerk*, sometimes used to conceal the larger pipes; it is found especially in the South Netherlands and was later developed also in South Germany.

This manner of distributing the different tonal departments of an organ is given the overall German title *Werkprinzip* (lit. 'work principle', using 'work' in the sense of a section or division) and, as has already been indicated, clearly identifies each *Werk* or section visually as well as aurally. Hence a trained observer, looking especially at a German or Dutch organ of any period between approximately 1500 and 1800, can usually tell from the instrument's appearance what its basic specification and tonal qualities are likely to be—that is, unless (and this is an important qualification) they have not been drastically altered at one time or another by restoration and/or rebuilding. It was not until the nineteenth century that entirely new conceptions of organ building led to the abandonment of this most logical and useful connection between visual and tonal apportionment and to which modern builders and designers have only recently returned.

In Germany, Austria and the Netherlands and, to a lesser extent, France, the range of pipes operated from the keyboards was, by *c.* 1500, reinforced by a range of lower-pitched pipes operated by pedals. This pedal section is revealed in casework by the presence of large side towers which are either an integral part of the original design or else are clearly later additions.

The early sixteenth-century late Gothic/Renaissance organ of these countries is a visual experience of great intensity, making its basic impact by the carefully planned arrangement and interaction of flats and towers. The oldest surviving cases of northern Europe are conceived in the light, soaring style associated with the ecclesiastical architecture of the later medieval Gothic era, the upthrust of the towers being emphasised by the rather rigid flats. More especially in Germany, the outline of the case often in fact recalls the castle rather than the church, perhaps because of the association with towers. (Though at Jutphaas in the Netherlands (6) actual miniature castles are carved round the top of the *cul-de-lampe*, or large decorative pendant.) The earlier Renaissance towers tend to take the pointed form on plan, but it was not long before rounded ones were introduced, and indeed seem always to have been more popular in France and the South Netherlands. (It is interesting to note that rounded towers are not strictly semicircular but for aesthetic and perspective reasons are normally slightly flattened.) At first terminating in lofty Gothic pinnacles, towers soon reflect the Renaissance preference for lantern-like structures on top; however, both these forms of tower decoration were eclipsed by the popularity of carved figures, amongst which those of musical angels, St Cecilia and King David were the first and most appropriate choice.

In both towers and flats the arrangement of the visible pipes was from an early date of crucial importance in helping to give interest and a sense of flow and movement to an organ front. As has already been explained, the usual Gothic solution was to place these pipes in a straight row along the impost, all having the same foot length. However, it is not length of foot which determines the pitch of a pipe, but the actual 'speaking length' between the mouth and the top. Thus organ builders and designers soon hit upon the idea of varying foot lengths in order to make the line produced by the level of pipe mouths more interesting. In a well designed organ pipe there is a basic aesthetic ratio between the length of the foot and that of the actual speaking length; as one increases the other should decrease, and vice versa. Designers of organ fronts began to make use of this principle in order to produce sequences of pipes whose mouths could then be arranged to form slopes or curves.

The lines formed by the pipe tops can be an equally important element in design—or rather, the concealment of those lines. The tops of a sequence of pipes produce a stepped effect whose contrast with other aspects of linear design may be too strong or too jagged. Early attempts to minimise this were made by inserting pieces of decorative carving in the spaces above the pipe tops (65, 66). Later this carving was sometimes made to follow the exact outline of the steps formed by the tops (72). Eventually the carved areas were brought down below the level of the pipe tops, which were then entirely concealed from view. These latter carvings are called pipe shades and, once the design principle had been established, could and did follow any line or take any form consistent with the overall design of the case. The only country where, with rare exceptions, they were never favoured was Italy, where designers traditionally preferred the pipes to stand unshaded. A form of inverted shade is sometimes found round the feet of organs in Germany and the Netherlands (74, 75).

Two other methods of arranging pipes remain to be mentioned. First, the toe board in which the feet of the pipes are inserted can itself be shaped, within limits, according to the designer's wishes, in order to vary still further the lines followed by the pipes. Secondly, an organ builder whose front design is liable to be spoiled by the inappropriate speaking lengths of pipes which he would otherwise wish to use, can cut away the tops of those pipes to produce the correct pitch whilst retaining a segment in front only, purely for the sake of the design.

The pipes on view in the front of a case are known as display pipes (less often, front or show pipes). They are almost invariably of metal—tin, lead, or a mixture of the two, itself known simply as 'metal'—and in the Gothic and Renaissance periods were often decorated by embossing or by gilding and/or painting (1, 5). A curious conceit was to single out the largest pipe in each tower for special decoration (10, 12). Originally display pipes were probably all speaking pipes, active members of the instrument's full complement of pipes, but as front designs became more complex dummy pipes were often used. The introduction of two or more tiers of pipes in both towers and flats can be traced back to the early fifteenth century (though in French designs towers remained in single tier). A speciality in the Netherlands was the arrangement of display pipes in a curious 'mirror' formation; these are in fact double pipes, each sounding the same note, the tone of which is thereby enriched (10, 12). Though some old organs retain their original display pipes, most have been replaced at one time or another; the expert can deduce their age to some extent by looking at the shape of the lips around the mouths, different forms of which have been preferred at different times.

The picture so far given has attempted to show the basic appearance of the organ at what many consider to have been the highest peak of its tonal and visual development. But the picture has in addition been restricted to those areas in which that development is held to have chiefly taken place—the Netherlands (both North and South), North Germany and France. Even within these areas there is no such thing as a standard organ case, though certain types are associated with certain builders (e.g. Arp Schnitger and the so-called 'Hamburg front'). Nor do the organs and their cases conform to rigid national boundaries, for at that period many organ builders were peripatetic; they travelled in areas rather than in specific countries, and this applies especially to the border lands of the various countries, where builders such as the members of the Schnitger and Silbermann families moved freely about. Furthermore, some immigrant builders either imported an alien style for isolated examples of cases, or else altered their own more typical styles to fit in with that of the country where they were working—yet seldom with complete success. However, the student of organ cases will soon find that there are certain national and regional characteristics which are an aid to identification, such as a French preference for round rather than pointed towers, or a South Netherlands addiction to clocks as a decorative feature.

Even more important is the fact that there are regional differences associated with certain countries that have to be taken into account. These countries are Spain, Italy and Britain. Spanish cases, many decisively influenced by those of Italy at the time of the Renaissance, are designed for the most part in tiered flats without the use of towers; where the latter are introduced, it is almost always as the result of outside influence or foreign workmanship (166, 186). In addition, Spanish cases received (mainly during the eighteenth century) a unique feature in the form of pipes arranged *en chamade*, i.e. projecting horizontally from the front of the instrument, so as to throw a powerful trumpet sound out into the building. Such pipes are seldom earlier than *c.* 1700.

Italian cases are in a class by themselves. Until the eighteenth century Italian organ builders were less interested than their North European counterparts in producing instruments with a wide range of tone colours, and the uniformly flat frontage of most classic Italian cases reflects this restraint, as does also the absence of any kind of *Positiv* division. Moreover, the typical Italian case, from its very beginnings, was designed according to the classical theories of the Italian Renaissance itself; these dictated a strongly architectural framework within which the pipes are disposed in a basic grouping in which three groups of large pipes arranged in pyramid formation are divided by two groups of double-tiered small pipes. There are many variations on this, especially in later examples, but on the whole the basic scheme remains remarkably constant. Equally constant is the framing of each group of pipes within a round-headed arch. There are no pipe shades, and until *c.* 1750 another universal feature was a wooden cross-piece or retaining bar placed across the front of each group of pipes (later they were secured from behind). Italian organ builders and designers alone maintained the old Gothic tradition of arranging the pipe mouths at the same level right across the front of the case.

In the unchanging tradition, over a long period of time, of the Italian organ case, it is possible to see a reflection of the unchanging Faith which the instrument itself served through all that time. The dangerously secular visual delights of the North European cases are avoided; in the same way the earlier Italian instruments were (until *c.* 1600) tonally orientated towards the vocal polyphony that was the musical mainstay of Catholic worship (comparatively little attempt being made to experiment with purely instrumental sound—hence the absence of the *Positiv* division in Italian organs), whilst in North Europe the various movements of the Reformation, though unfortunately leading to the spoliation or destruction of many organs, ultimately changed the musical and liturgical rôle of the organ, and in so doing gave organ builders freedom to develop and introduce much wider schemes of tone colour which are reflected in the *Werkprinzip* cases.

The organ in Britain differed primarily from other North European types in that it had no independent pedal section until the eighteenth century; hence British cases were on the whole smaller. Owing to the destructive havoc wrought first at the Reformation and then during the Commonwealth period, very few genuine pre-Restoration (1660) cases remain. One British peculiarity is that the *Positiv* section is nowadays called the *Choir*. Modern research has shown that this term has nothing to do with singing, but is a corruption of an earlier spelling, *Chaire*, perhaps referring to the organist's bench incorporated within the back of the *Positiv* case. A more probable though less obvious explanation relates to an old English verb 'to chair', meaning to turn to, or to take a hand at something (hence, 'charwoman'); in this sense the organist used to turn aside to the positive organ before it was actually incorporated within the main organ.

Styles of Decoration

As has already been shown, the form and decoration of the earliest organ cases are both closely associated with the ecclesiastical style of the later Middle Ages, the Gothic. This is a style sufficiently well known for further explanation to be unnecessary at this point. There is perhaps less general confidence about the Renaissance and its artistic manifestations.

The movement known generally since the nineteenth century as the Renaissance (but originally as 'the New Learning') began effectively in Italy in *c.* 1420. In the field of architecture the Renaissance sought to restore the balance, harmony and basic simplicity of Classical ideals, while the elements of its decoration also derived ultimately from ancient Roman sources. An enquiring, all-embracing humanism (exemplified at its best in the work and person of Leonardo da Vinci) replaced the spiritual mysticism and sheer blind faith of the Middle Ages.

In organ-case design it is not surprising that this new approach first appears in Italy where, as noted above, the earliest cases built on the new principles set a basic type which was seldom deviated from in that country for several hundred years. In North Europe, however, it is not the form of the case (based as it was on the non-Italian idea of the *Werkprinzip*) but the decorative elements which indicate Renaissance influence. These elements may be divided basically into (a) geometrical squares and lozenge shapes known as strapwork and printed in Flemish pattern books of the period (46, 47, 49); (b) carved three-dimensional portrait heads (2, 3, 8, 44); (c) grotesques—this term covers a multitude of devices including animal and floral forms, human faces and abstract designs, all conceived in a thin, linear style (derived from Roman interior decoration) that is seen to best advantage—as might be expected—in Italian cases (207–211, 215 etc.) but is also found in North European examples (10, 69, 70, 125). Obviously (a) and (b) are more usually associated with the casework of the substructure, whilst the linear qualities of (c) make it ideal for decoration on cornices, inter-flat divisions, and similar areas. The Renaissance is above all a secular style, and we may be surprised by the evident ease with which it found its way into churches and cathedrals, not infrequently via the organ case.

To the art historian the High Renaissance properly ends in 1527 with the Sack of Rome, and Renaissance style is then metamorphosed into an exaggerated version known as Mannerism; this prevailed until *c.* 1600 when it was replaced by the Baroque. The identification of Mannerism need not concern the student of organ cases too closely, although it undoubtedly influenced the decoration of certain cases. The Baroque, however, is a highly important element in case design, although in earlier examples it is not always immediately obvious and moreover at this period is often linked with Renaissance elements as well (47). Its progress can be usefully traced in the increasing size and realism of the three-dimensional carved figures which now tended almost universally (in North Europe) to replace the crowning lanterns favoured by designers for the tops of towers. We have referred earlier to St Cecilia, King David, and their attendant angels; it is worth noting that the wide selection of musical instruments played by the latter are sometimes represented with considerable accuracy (116), but are more often mere stereotypes and if real would in fact be unplayable.

Baroque artists and designers threw off the restraints that had been imposed upon them by the classical disciplines of the Renaissance and allowed their imaginations far greater freedom; following the example of the great Bernini (1598–1680), they used painting and sculpture together to produce works of mixed composition, they enlisted into their service the age-old devices of perspective and *trompe l'œil* to deceive the eye of the beholder (36, 39, 66, 244), and they strove to achieve the illusion of realism in whatever medium they happened to be using. A subsidiary manifestation of the style is a certain perverseness which sets out to make wood look like stone, marble like drapery, and so on. Something of the same spirit also shows itself in the Baroque partiality for 'toy' stops imitating the sounds of cuckoo, nightingale, drum, etc, for the *Cymbelstern* stop (a gilded star with little bells at its tips that not only ornamented the organ case but could be activated by a drawstop and made to revolve, causing the bells to set up a delicate carillon), and for curious mechanical devices such as moving human heads with rolling eyes and lolling tongues, or the ox at Ochsenhausen (79). The nature of its construction imposes upon an organ—and hence on its case also—a vertical rigidity which must in the last resort be maintained, even in the most extreme examples of Baroque flamboyance such as the case at Weingarten (83). Given this fact, designers—above all, those of Germany and Austria—sought to conceal the actual lines of their cases, or at least to distract the viewer's attention sufficiently from them, by a welter of applied carved and/or painted ornament in which realistic three-dimensional figures and luxuriantly carved, pierced and gilded pipe shades have pride of place (74, 75, 79, 80, 82, 87). Straining Atlas figures labour to support the gigantic mass, exuberant side-pieces—likewise carved and often pierced—replace the wings or folding shutters now rendered obsolete by the increased complexity of case fronts. In some Spanish and later Italian organs this extravagance becomes positively embarassing (181, 185, 236, 238, 239, 241).

The mid-eighteenth century Rococo style, whilst at first sight indistinguishable from the Baroque in its extravagance, is in fact based mainly on naturalistic motifs (fruit, flowers, animals and birds) and also on a device known as the C-scroll, from its resemblance to that letter. The keynote of the style is lightness (emphasised by much use of white and gold paint) and a certain frivolity, and under its influence designers of organ cases came as near as they had ever done to abandoning the traditional outlines altogether (91, 92, 98, 100, 102, 104). It is found at its best in South Germany, Austria and the adjoining areas of Switzerland, where a merrier religious spirit—akin to that of Italy—on the whole prevails than in the more dourly Protestant parts of North Europe. The essence of the Rococo can perhaps best be fancifully though not inappropriately expressed in culinary terms: while a Baroque organ case may remind one of a large, over-rich fruit cake, a Rococo case is an altogether lighter concoction, frothed up, sugared, and topped with cream. The fluidity of the Rococo style enabled designers to carry still further the principle already established under the influence of the Baroque—that of moulding cases to their architectural setting, so as to create a fusion between the two (86, 92, 95, 102).

The Neo-classical movement of the later eighteenth century produced a few interesting experiments in case design (201), and at least one awful warning (153). The succeeding Gothic Revival, however, is almost totally devoid of any kind of visual interest. There are of course one or two notable exceptions to this (41, 66, 264), but on the whole the few examples shown in this book are enough to illustrate the apparently almost complete lack of appreciation which the designers of the earlier nineteenth century had of the work of their medieval counterparts, whom they professed to imitate.

Siting

We cannot leave this general discussion of the organ case without some reference to its siting, for this aspect too has had an important effect on design over the centuries.

Large Gothic organs were normally erected in specially constructed galleries or in lofts, of which the most visually attractive form is the so-called 'swallow's nest' type (4, 65). It was probably mainly the growing size of organs that soon forced this type out of general favour. Sometimes, however, organs were suspended high up on the wall of nave or transept, hanging thence apparently almost in mid-air and without visible means of support (126). The engineering skill required for this feat was necessarily considerable even by today's standards. A high placing of course results in wide diffusion of sound, and this might be thought to have been a disadvantage in liturgical use. In fact it was not, for in the various countries of North Europe the main organ was not normally used for the accompaniment of congregational singing until the Reformation—indeed, until then there was little or no congregational singing at all. For choral accompaniment most large churches had one or more smaller organs placed at strategic points about the building. Even after the Reformation some of the more extreme sects restricted the use of the organ to preludes and postludes, and to regular recitals unconnected with the church services. This is especially noticeable in the North Netherlands, where the organ often belonged to the town rather than the church in which it stood (and still does, e.g. at Haarlem), and where civic pride and rivalry was frequently reflected in the efforts of various town councils to commission the building of larger and more imposing organs than their neighbours, often from the same builder.

There are a number of instances of surviving Gothic galleries supporting organs of later date (123). The most strikingly successful overall compositions of organ-cum-gallery (and sometimes the screen beneath as well) are of course those planned from the start by just one designer as a single entity (13, 22, 48). Where the gallery, having been originally an integral part of the design, has later been removed, the composition is noticeably spoiled (73).

Although during the Gothic period a position on the north wall of church or cathedral was traditional, a west-end siting for the main organ has long been favoured in Germany and France (though in certain areas of North Germany there is a Lutheran tradition—not illustrated in this book—of uniting altar, pulpit and organ in a single composition at the east end). From c. 1550 this position was also generally adopted in the Netherlands, although in Flanders there seems to have been a vogue during the seventeenth and eighteenth centuries of placing organs on choir screens. As the instruments of North Europe grew larger the west end probably offered the one suitable wall area which still afforded scope for upward growth. On occasion the selection of this siting for the organ clashed with the need to allow light to enter the church through the west window, and there were a number of interesting architectural solutions to this problem (69).

Once again Spain, Italy and to a certain extent Britain deviated from the norm. In Spain the highly developed tradition of antiphonal singing and the liturgical convention of an enclosed choir in the centre of a monastic church, rather than at the east end, frequently led to the building of two facing organs. They are usually identified as being on the 'Epistle' or 'Gospel' side of the sanctuary (on the right and left respectively as one faces the altar), taking the terms from the liturgical positions established for the readings of the New Testament during the Mass. The cases of these organs had to be double-fronted, since they faced into the side-aisles as well as into the choir, and they had also to be tall and narrow, because of the need to fit them between the nave arches. (The narrowness of these cases may have contributed, at least in part, to the specifically Spanish feature of exterior pipes arranged *en chamade*, space within the cases being at a premium.) However, the tradition of double organs in no way precluded the use of other sitings in Spain, especially in smaller or non-monastic churches.

In Italy a similar antiphonal tradition is again frequently expressed in terms of identical cases facing each other across the church. On occasion one of these is found to be a dummy. Some free-standing organs placed under arches have double fronts, as in Spain (205, 206, 222, 223). Where there is only one organ its traditional position is in a gallery, at one or other side of the altar; apse or transept sitings are less frequent, and west end ones not normally found before the eighteenth century.

In Britain the preference in many of the larger churches and cathedrals was for a position on the choir screen. Consequently the double-fronted case occurred in a ratio of greater frequency than on the Continent, with the exception of Spain. Moreover the presence of the *Chaire* case (not paralleled in Spain) gave added interest to the composition.

It should never be forgotten that in a large number of instances organs have been moved from their original positions, some more than once; some, indeed, are no longer even in their original homes, as many entries in this book will show.

The Makers

To conclude this short introduction a word should be said about the men who made the organs and their cases. (Indeed the original term for an organ builder was 'organ maker'.) We may for convenience divide the categories of organs as follows:

1. Those designed and built throughout, case and instrument, by the same man.
2. Those in which the case was provided by a practical joiner or cabinet-maker, working independently of the organ builder who supplied the instrument, though in consultation with him.
3. Those in which the case was designed by an architect.

In each of these categories the adornment of the case, whether carving and/or painting, is very often known to have been executed by professionals.

Summarised lists of the names of the various organ builders, craftsmen, painters, carvers and architects mentioned in the captions will be found at the back of this book. The list of craftsmen known to have been employed is almost as long as that of the organ builders themselves, and there are obviously many instances where the names of the craftsmen have been lost. When building a large instrument an organ builder would of necessity subcontract part of the work, and as early as 1475 the contract for Chartres stipulates that the builder is to provide all the necessary timber, carvings, heraldic achievements, painting and gilding (though not, curiously enough, the metal for the pipes). In theory the medieval system of the trade guilds, whilst it lasted, prevented the organ builder from making his own cases, which were considered the province of the joiner or cabinet-maker. In practice, however, and especially where smaller instruments were concerned, these restrictions were often ignored. Certain organ builders regularly worked in conjunction with certain craftsmen; for example, there were fruitful partnerships between Nicolaes Niehoff and Jan Schalken (45), and between Arp Schnitger and Allart Meijer (19, 22).

There are magnificent organ cases specially designed by architects, such as Jacob van Kampen's case at Alkmaar or Christopher Wren's case in St Paul's Cathedral, London. On the other hand there are equally magnificent and striking cases apparently the unaided design of organ builders, such as those by Joseph Gabler at Weingarten or Karl Joseph Riepp at Ottobeuren. The names of certain builders are linked with specific types of design, such as Arp Schnitger's 'Hamburg front', the wide designs of J.-B. Forceville, or the 'Liège' type developed by the Flemish school. Some of the finest and most attractive cases remain anonymous to this day. However, it is hoped that in the following pages the names of many excellent artists and craftsmen, little known and long forgotten, will live again, and that fresh honour may be done to those whose names are already rightly celebrated in the annals of organ building.

Captions to the Plates

Netherlands (North)

MIDDELBURG Koorkerk

Originally built in 1479 by Peter Gerritsz of Utrecht for the Sint-Nicolaaskerk in that city, 1–3
and now the oldest surviving organ in Holland. The outlines of the main case (whose front
was then flat) already show the established form of a housing for keyboard and mechanism
surmounted by a much wider and larger superstructure containing the pipes.

Between 1547 and 1580 alterations were carried out which radically altered the organ's
appearance, as well as enlarging its tonal capacities. These involved (a) the addition of a
V-shaped central tower, to accommodate larger pipes; (b) the inclusion of new ranks of pipes
displayed in the central flat, some of them in 'mirror' formation; (c) the addition of a *Positief*
consisting of three conjoined V-shaped towers.

In the decorative carving of the *Positief* the Renaissance elements present a clear contrast
to the more delicate abstract tracery of the High Gothic portions of the main case. These
Renaissance elements include typical grotesques and human portrait heads, some of which
may be studied in detail in plates 2 and 3. The same plates also show details of the geometrical
diamond-type embossing which is to be found on the pipes of both the earlier and later parts
of the organ.

In 1885 the organ was taken to the Rijksmuseum in Amsterdam and in 1951 to Middelburg,
where it is now. It was probably during one or other of these moves that the original wings
(whose hinges are still to be seen on the main case) were removed.

ALKMAAR Sint-Laurenskerk (Grote Kerk)

The smaller of the two famous instruments at Alkmaar, this was built in 1511 by Jan van 4
Covelen (Johann von Koblenz) and enlarged in 1555 by Allaert Claesz of Haarlem. It
is to be found on the north wall of the ambulatory, in an elegant and highly decorative
'swallow's nest' gallery whose original proportions were somewhat spoiled by the 1555
alterations.

The equally decorative case reflects the final phase of Gothic in the diversity and richness of
its carved ornament, including the tower crowns, and the challenging new complexity—
necessarily echoed by the shutters—of its five-part front with three towers and two double-
storeyed flats. Indeed some experts attribute to van Covelen himself the introduction of
towers, both round and pointed, into Netherlands case design; if this is so the Alkmaar organ
is of especial significance, the more so since it demonstrates the use of both types of tower in a
single front.

AMSTERDAM Rijksmuseum

Built in 1526 by Johannes Emedensis (probably Johan Molner of Emden), removed from its 5
original home church at Scheemda (Groningen) in 1874, and the empty case bought for the
Rijksmuseum in 1896.

Though later than the 1511 Alkmaar instrument, this case is in the earlier Gothic tradition of a totally flat front whose lines are a judicious mixture of formality and beautiful fluidity, the latter being emphasised by carved tendrils of great delicacy and vivacity. Though there are no towers, the three main pipe compartments are carried upward, as it were, by the carving above them. The pipes themselves are all diapered and embossed; the sloping and V-arrangements of the mouths are unusual in Gothic instruments, and suggest that alterations may have been made when the case was set up in the Museum. With its outstretched wings the whole case gives a notable impression of a medieval triptych.

Painting forms an important feature of this case. Not only are the wings painted on both sides (exterior: the Tree of Jesse; interior: scenes from the Nativity), but these are keyed into the main design of the case by painted corbels which support the superstructure. The slightly grotesque treatment of the trumpet-blowing heads painted on these, as also of the two quaint figures carved in the openwork panels above the drawstops, seems to be Renaissance rather than Gothic in inspiration. The heraldic shields supported by the two latter figures bear devices including, respectively, three organ pipes and a plane; it has been suggested that the figures represent the organ builder and his assistant (or possibly the joiner who made the case).

JUTPHAAS   Sint-Nicolaas

6   A late Gothic *tour-de-force* which, however, has undergone changes since its original beginnings *c.* 1520 in the Nieuwe Zijds Kapel at Amsterdam (the builder may have been Jan van Covelen again), where it was situated in a 'swallow's nest' against the north wall. After several alterations at different times it was finally taken down in 1871 to make way for a new instrument. Fortunately the case was preserved for posterity by the enthusiasm of Gerard Willem van Heukelum, a noted Dutch Gothic Revivalist of the period, who saw the case as the focal decorative point of the new church which he was then designing for Jutphaas, and of which he eventually became the parish priest.

Less fortunately, the case was placed (1879) in a gallery with a window, where it necessarily loses some of the impact that would otherwise have been provided by a solid wall behind, since its delicate silhouette does not show up to such good advantage. Restoration of the case itself was carried out by Wilhelm Mengelberg, a sculptor, who among other alterations is known to have shortened considerably the two rounded towers at each side; these, it seems, were originally taller than the front tower. However, there is still enough of the original case left for us to marvel at this Gothic extravaganza culminating in a central octagonal structure like a monstrance or reliquary.

It could be said that the organ's ornate design detracts from its functional appearance as a musical instrument. Despite this, a careful appraisal will reveal its similarity to the organ front at Alkmaar (4), although at Jutphaas the sequence of U–V–U towers is reversed and there are additional towers at the sides. Yet the most interesting and unusual feature of all is the way in which the organ has taken on the type of design, appearance and siting more usually associated with a *Positief*.

New shutters, probably replacing the original ones, were painted in the early seventeenth century by Jan Asselijn, and these were placed by van Heukelum in the Aartsbisschoppelijk Museum at Utrecht, founded by himself.

MONNIKENDAM   Nederlandse Hervormde Kerk

7   At first sight this organ appears to be of the same type and period as those at Alkmaar and Jutphaas; indeed, in its original state it dates from the same period as the latter and may even be the work of Jan van Covelen. However, a closer inspection reveals a number of decorative

inconsistencies, and these are mainly accounted for by a reconstruction of some magnitude carried out in 1780–1.

Most noticeable is the non-Gothic manner in which the display flats have been divided up, with the pipes in the upper compartments standing in slopes. The heavy openwork carving of the pipe shades is in the late eighteenth-century manner, as are also the trophies of musical instruments painted on the shutters (not the original wooden ones, but replacements of cloth stretched on wooden frames). It is, however, possible to admire the considerable skill and restraint with which the eighteenth century has managed to merge itself reasonably well with the original Gothic without in any way resorting to pastiche.

The organ was moved from the traditional position on the north wall to one at the west end as early as 1639.

ENKHUIZEN   Sint-Gommaruskerk (Westerkerk)
Dated 1547 on the *Positief*, the usual ascription is to Hendrik Niehoff, and there are indeed   8, 9
indications of Niehoff's style in the tiered flats, the double-tiered central tower, the two V-shaped towers projecting over flats and the U–V–U–V–U arrangement of the *Positief*. All these elements can be found in Niehoff's famous 1551–2 organ at the Sankt Johanniskirche, Lüneburg (Germany), where even the elaborate three-tiered triple lanterns are echoed though not precisely copied.

The Renaissance-inspired decoration at Enkhuizen is at its most evident in the carved human heads protruding from triangular pediments and in the curious bulbous pendants at the base of the *Positief*. The cunningly contrived and intricate vaulting beneath the *Positief* is especially notable, though its effect is somewhat marred and its outline blurred by the later additions of volutes (carved in relief with musical instruments) which link it to the doorframe.

The black and gold colours in which the organ is now painted, though striking, are not original.

ABCOUDE   Sint-Cosmas-en-Damianus
Built originally by Hendrik Niehoff for the Sint-Janskerk at Gouda in 1556–8, moved to the   10
Lutheran church there in 1744, and only the case and display pipes taken thereafter to Abcoude, together with part of the original parapet (1904).

The instrument did not survive these moves unscathed. The shutters have vanished. The proportions of the main case have suffered through the removal of the original pipes in the central double-tiered tower and its conversion to a single tier containing pipes whose larger proportions spoil the effect of the whole. The supporting structure of the main case has been drastically cut down and the *Positief* no longer fulfils its original design function, since it has been placed far too low down in relation to the main case (both cases are empty). However, many interesting features remain, in particular the wealth of Renaissance-style carving, the 'mirror' arrangement of pipes in the lower flats of both the main and *Positief* cases, and the embossing of the largest pipe in each tower(except the main one). The colouring is not original.

LOPPERSUM   Nederlandse Hervormde Kerk
The date 1562, inscribed on this case, is misleading; alterations took place in the eighteenth,   11
nineteenth and twentieth centuries before the latest restoration in 1965 (during which this photograph was taken; hence the missing pipe shades of the *Positief*). As a result of the latter changes the instrument now approximates once again to its original general appearance. In detail, however, it is much changed. From the sixteenth century there remain the canopies of the three main towers, the seven pipes in the central tower, and the gallery parapet. The small Atlas figures beneath the main impost, and the bell-ringing figure at the right of the main

substructure, may also be of the Renaissance. The device of flame-like tongues between the pipe feet is associated more with the Baroque period (cf. 112, 116), while the elaborate carved and chequered side-pieces with their trumpet-blowing figures are of the eighteenth century, as is also the carving round the cornice of the *Positief*. The classical urns and unsightly medallion on top of the case date from a rebuild of 1802–3, as the medallion itself proclaims. On the other hand, the original gilded texts and much of the original colouring have been restored.

's-HERTOGENBOSCH   Kathedraal van Sint-Jan

12 Though the original instrument within it was not completed until 1635, the case was completed by the Tyrolean craftsman Georg Schysler in 1618.

Built on the plan –v–u–v– (echoed by the *Positief*), with double-tiered towers in the main case, this front is a textbook of typical Renaissance ornament ranging from human heads and grotesques carved in relief and openwork to the three-dimensional figures of musicians carved below the impost, between the two subsidiary V towers of the main front, and on the heavy superstructure itself; the latter also bears a carving of that most typical of Renaissance motifs, the Dance of Death, and points the moral of the passage of time by its culmination in a clock.

The division between towers and flats in both the main case and the *Positief* is here made by means of columns, classical on the main case but in the *Positief* twisted in the 'barley sugar' manner which heralds the approach of the Baroque. In the main towers each largest pipe is chased and gilded, according to custom, and in the intervening flats the conceit of 'mirror' pipes is again employed.

Some experts see this case as the supreme example of Renaissance architecture. For others it is spoiled by what they see as the excessive emphasis on the superstructure.

ALKMAAR   Sint-Laurenskerk (Grote Kerk)

13 Through the recordings made by Helmut Walcha this has become one of the best-known organs in western Europe. It certainly has one of the most satisfying cases of the period, a happy circumstance which owes much to its having been designed all of a piece—together with the whole structure of the gallery from floor upwards—by the architect Jacob van Campen, who later built the Town Hall of Amsterdam.

The main organ case was built during the years 1638–43, and van Campen was assisted in general planning and design by the painter Pieter Jansz Saenredam, the actual making of the case being carried out by the cabinet-maker Jacob Jansz Turck. The severity implied by the classical elements of columns, pilasters and (surmounting and unifying the whole case) pediment is offset by the exuberant Baroque carvings of putti, musical instruments and, more especially, fruit and flowers; in particular, the heavy swags above the cornice recall the Dutch still-life flower paintings of the period. Three Dutch artists were in fact associated with the decoration of the shutters; these were painted on the inside by Adriaan Valk and Hendrik Gebrandsz with figures of St Cecilia and King David, and on the outside by Caspar van Everdingen with a single scene of David and Saul returning from their victory over the Philistines.

Somewhat unusually for a Dutch organ of this period, there are no pointed towers, the arrangements being –u–u–u–; however, the outermost flats, being extremely narrow, can be regarded almost as flattened extensions of the outer towers, more especially since each is mirrored on the other side of the tower.

The *Positief* was not part of van Campen's original design, but was added later after a design by Dirck Thomasz, an employee of the organ builder Germer van Hagebeer of Amersfoort, who built the actual instrument in 1641–6. The *Positief* (which has since lost its shutters) complements the main case sufficiently gracefully, though it is perhaps not improved by the carved groups of children flanking a centrepiece consisting of a coiled serpent with tail in mouth. The modern visitor may be forgiven for failing to note in this an allegorical reference to the unity of the Seven Provinces.

Hagebeer's work was largely altered in 1723–5 by Franz Caspar Schnitger of Zwolle, and as a musical instrument it is for Schnitger's specification and distinctive tone (both carefully restored in recent years by D. A. Flentrop of Zandaam) that the organ is famed today.

ZEERIJP   Nederlandse Hervormde Kerk
Built 1645–53 by Theodor Faber, presumably a German. This case is noteworthy for its late   14
Renaissance carved and openwork tower crownings, for the manner in which the outer towers of the *Positief* are angled, and for the fact that the central tower of the main case is cut off short, as it were, allowing space for the insertion of a cartouche recording the dedication of the organ in 1651 and flanked by two *Cymbelsterne*.

After several alterations and repairs over a period of some 250 years, the original instrument almost entirely vanished during a rebuild in 1933, when the present display pipes were also put in. However, during restoration of the church in 1966 the dark colouring of the case (as shown in the photograph) was removed, to reveal the original plain oak with gilt carvings and the shutters of blue, grey and gold.

DORDRECHT   Onze-Lieve-Vrouwekerk (Grote Kerk)
By Nicolaes van Haeghen of Antwerp, completed 1671. With its large tower-caps, a high and   15
largely plain substructure, short central towers and flats, and in its general appearance, the main case is reminiscent of English cases of the period, in particular those of Bernard Smith who is thought to have spent his formative years in the Netherlands and/or Germany until returning to England at the Restoration in 1660. The heraldic devices surmounting the towers are those of the town, burgomaster and churchwardens, a typical expression of civic pride common to many organs in Holland where often the organ is the property of the town and not of the church in which it stands.

During the eighteenth century additions to the case were made in the Rococo style, admirable in themselves but deplorable when grafted onto the taste of an earlier age. Particularly unfortunate are the vase-like supports beneath the pedal towers, the C-scroll volutes at the sides of the main case, and the side-pieces added to the *Positief*.

MEDEMBLIK   Nederlandse Hervormde Kerk
Original instrument by Pieter E. Backer, built 1668–71, case by Jacob Dirckz Laechlant II,   16
carvings by Jan Meegh, and shutters (now gone) painted and gilded by Adrijaan Spanjaert. Moved from the north to the west wall of the church in 1859, this, though small, is perhaps the most obviously 'vertical' example of all the Netherlands organ cases in this book, probably because the main case is not much wider than the *Positief* beneath it (although the latter may have been slightly enlarged during the eighteenth century).

Based on a simple v–u–v plan, the lines of the case inevitably lead the eye upwards until it rests on the carved harp-playing figure of King David supported by cornett-blowing boys, pinnacles, the civic arms, and heaps of appetising-looking fruit. This whole group is the most significant remnant of Jan Meegh's carvings; the trophy of musical instruments and trumpeting figures of the *Positief* seem to be later (probably eighteenth century), as are also the carved side-pieces on both the main and *Positief* cases which took the place of the original shutters.

Struck by lightning in 1861, the organ survived the ordeal, and was last restored (by D. A. Flentrop) in 1966.

AMSTERDAM Waalse Kerk

17 From about 1575 a number of French Protestants settled in Holland and formed their own church there. In Amsterdam they were granted the use of an old church in 1586, and in 1680 (the first year in which organs were permitted to be used for congregational accompaniment in Holland) this organ was built. The tradition that it was the work of Nicolas Langlez of Tournai is reinforced by the design of the main case, which is not traditionally North Holland but in the so-called 'Liège' style; this is characterised by the single central tower supported by flats whose height decreases successively and the outermost of which curve slightly backwards (see also 44, 46, 48, 49). The carved decoration is rich in cornucopiae, swags and fantastic creatures, piled up sequentially with the fragmented curvilinear pediments to culminate in a graceful vase. Originally two-tiered, the flats were reduced to single tiers in 1733–4.

The *Positief* is less striking in shape and decoration (though the relief carving is delicate enough), and moreover has been spoiled during the eighteenth century by the removal of the original crown and its substitution by a central musical instrument trophy supported by female figures.

In 1891 the case was painted brown, in accordance with the taste of those times. A restoration carried out in 1963–5 by Ahrend and Brunzema of Leer, Germany, included the replacement of the original shutters (probably also removed in 1891) with new ones, and repainting and gilding in the original colours.

AMSTERDAM Westerkerk

18 The builder of this 1686 instrument, Jan Duyschot, repeated the same basic design of v–u–v towers and tiered flats in two other organs, the one now at Middelburg (20, 21) and in the Nieuwe Kerk at The Hague. Here at Amsterdam the casework was executed by Jan Jansz, who has surmounted the main case with figures of Faith, Hope and Charity; beneath the *Positief* an especially fine floral swag is held by carved angels. The main shutters, of cloth stretched on wooden frames, bear paintings on the inside of King David and of Solomon and the Queen of Sheba, by Gerard de Lairesse; the paintings on the outside have now vanished, probably at a time when the shutters were removed and almost sold. The *Positief* shutters have also been removed but are still to be seen in the church; these were decorated, also by Lairesse, with figures of the Evangelists on the outer surfaces and with trophies of musical instruments on the inner.

The manner in which both the main case and its gallery are supported at the the front by classical columns and pilasters is repeated elsewhere in Holland, notably at Alkmaar (13).

GRONINGEN Martinikerk (Grote Kerk)

19 The main case is still basically that of the 1542 instrument built by Andreas de Mare. The *Positief*, however, was designed in 1729–30 by a local architect, A. Verburg, to replace a case of 1480 which de Mare had used for his own *Positief*. The pipe shades and other carvings on the main case present typical Renaissance grotesques, fantastic animals, portrait medallions and the like; the display pipes are also of this period.

For an important 1691–2 rebuild by Arp Schnitger the cabinet-maker Allart Meijer provided the two large side towers, into which were fitted a number of the pipes from Schnitger's new 32-foot *Praestant* pedal stop (the only remaining complete example of a displayed 32-foot stop by this builder). Pedal towers in this form were new to Holland at the time, and Meijer has astutely linked them to the main case by two-tier flats of dummy pipes. The influence of the Baroque may be seen in the manner in which one arm of each of the trumpet-playing figures in the pipe shades is carved three-dimensionally.

During the mid-nineteenth century the case was painted mahogany and gilded.

MIDDELBURG   Nieuwe Kerk

Though also by Jan Duyschot (1692) and based on the same design as that used at the   20, 21
Amsterdam Westerkerk six years earlier (18), this case is more assertive in that the curves and
angles of the main case towers are more pronounced and the central tower stands proud of the
supporting towers and flats, without being linked to them as at Amsterdam. As a result of
this the curved pediment is more compressed and emphatic. The case itself was made by Jan
Albertsz Schut and the carving executed by Jasper Wagenaar and possibly also by Symon
Muller, although the female figures surmounting the main outer flats may be of earlier date
and from another case.

The shutters were probably painted by Philip Tidemann of Hamburg, pupil and assistant
of Gerard de Lairesse. The larger pair are of cloth on frames, bearing on the exterior scenes
from the Nativity and on the interior Jepthah (left) and David and Saul (right). The
smaller pair are of wood and decorated with allegorical subjects. On both pairs the exteriors
are painted in grisaille (monochrome imitation of sculpture), the interiors in colour. Paintings
also appear on the substructure—an unusual feature. The overhang is again supported on
classical columns, as at Alkmaar and the Amsterdam Westerkerk (13, 18).

The quality of the carving can be studied in greater detail in plate 21. It will be noticed
that the motif beneath the *Positief* of a floral swag supported by angels is repeated (cf. 18),
although here the central angel of the Westerkerk becomes two angels, one bearing an open
book and the other a stringed instrument.

In 1884 the case was removed from the Oude Lutherse Kerk in Amsterdam, for which it was
originally built, and installed in the Rijksmuseum (plate 20 dates from this period). In 1951
it was sold to Middelburg and a new instrument was built into it by Willem van Leeuwen of
Leiderdorp.

GRONINGEN   A-Kerk

The flat/wide impression conveyed by this case is not typical of Dutch organs of this or indeed   22
any other period, and in fact the instrument is by Arp Schnitger, built 1699–1702 originally
for the Minderbroederskerk and moved to its present location in 1815.

The case, gallery and screen were executed for Schnitger by his frequent collaborator the
cabinet-maker Allart Meijer. Typical of Schnitger's designs are the double-tiered flats all of
equal size, the faceted tower caps and supports, and the carved openwork side-pieces. The
Positief is a smaller edition of the main case.

During the move of 1815 certain unfortunate changes were made to the case. These mainly
involved removal of the typical openwork tower crowns and their replacement by unnatur-
ally elongated figures, while two Atlas figures were added beneath the main end-towers.
Probably at the same time the all-important overhang of the main case was cut back, while in
1857 the proportions of the case were further spoiled by the enlargement of the substructure
so as to accommodate more pipework.

CULEMBORG   Sint-Barbarakerk (Grote Kerk)

Built in 1719 by M. Verhofstad, this elegant case introduces us to a type especially favoured in   23
the South Netherlands, in which the main case is brought forward to the front of the gallery,
as it were absorbing the *Positief* into itself; the keyboards are now at the back of the case.

The carving of the pipe shades and vertical posts is especially striking, and there are fine
acanthus *culs-de-lampe* beneath the two main end-towers and that of the *Positief* (in this and
cases of similar design officially known as an *Onderwerk*). The figure of King David and the
two flanking vases are less successful and in any case seem to be of later date. Also probably

later are the curious *trompe l'œil* additions to the sides of the case, which may have been added to replace the original shutters, if there were any.

It may be noted in passing that whilst rounded towers are more typical generally of the French and South Netherlands schools of case design, their popularity as against that of pointed ones increased as the angularities of the Renaissance softened into the curves of the Baroque and Rococo styles.

ZWOLLE   Sint-Michaëlskerk (Grote Kerk)

24   Completed in 1721 by Johann Jürgen and Franz Caspar Schnitger who based their work on a plan drawn up in 1718 by their father Arp Schnitger (d. 1719). The case, however, was designed on mainly traditional Dutch lines by Jurriaan Westerman, a sculptor of Amsterdam, who provided the carved figures including probably that of King David, whose position in the lower tier of the central tower, replacing display pipes, is unusual.

The preponderance on this case of large carved figures, including angels, musicians and Atlases, is in fact rather remarkable. It may already have been observed, in some of the preceding plates, how frequently one meets with two female figures (often, as here, on top of the *Positief* outer towers), one with a stringed musical instrument, the other holding a book or scroll. The usual interpretation is that these figures represent Music and Poetry respectively; they appear to be a traditional feature of case design in the North Netherlands, though not so frequently encountered as the figures of David and St Cecilia. The painting and gilding here were done by Anthoni Aardewijn.

's-GRAVENHAGE   Oud-Katholieke Kerk

25   Completed in 1724 by the North German organ builder Rudolph Garrels, the case much influenced in its decoration by the French Baroque style in which the rest of the church is also ornamented. This is perhaps most noticeable in the impressive carved trophies of musical instruments which form the side-pieces. The carved figures of angels are over-large, particularly that sitting on top of the *Positief* (on which the lyres are also typically French); the size of this figure perhaps represents an attempt to compensate for the absence (owing to lack of space) of any kind of crowning or superstructure above the towers.

AMSTERDAM   Oude Kerk

26   Designed by Jurriaan Westerman to contain an instrument by Christian Vater completed in 1726. The similarity to Westerman's design for the Sint-Michaelskerk at Zwolle (24) is plain to see. However, here at Amsterdam the curves and points of the main case towers are less marked, and the central tower has display pipes in both tiers, while the main division between the tiers comes two-thirds up the front instead of halfway as at Zwolle. In addition, the outermost flats as well as the inner are here divided into three.

Here too there is happily less emphasis on heavy carved figures, although those of Music and Poetry are repeated (in somewhat different form) on the *Positief*. But the overall proportions of the Amsterdam case, which is noticeably broader, are perhaps less good than those at Zwolle, and the clock is not a happy feature.

LEENS   Nederlandse Hervormde Kerk

27   The builder of this organ (*c.* 1735), Albert Anthoni Hinsz, was successor to Franz Caspar Schnitger, having been his foreman.

Little can be said in favour of the general appearance of this organ, except perhaps for the *Positief*, whose proportions are reasonably pleasing. The tower crowns, though found on other Schnitger and Schnitger-type organs in this area of Holland (Groningen), are clumsy and heavy, though to be fair one must allow that their squat appearance here may have been to some extent dictated by the low roof. In placing a carving of King David in the lower tier of the central tower Hinsz was no doubt following the example of Westerman at Zwolle (24); here, however, the figure is so meagre as to be pathetic. But most unpleasing of all to the eye is the manner in which the organ rises up out of the welter of heraldic carvings on the gallery like an ornament in a garden rockery.

New display pipes were fitted in 1924.

GOUDA   Sint-Janskerk (Grote Kerk)
Case designed in 1732 by the painter Hendrik Carré and carved by Dirk van der Wagt, to   28
contain an instrument by Jacob François Moreau of Rotterdam.

In appearance this is not a typical Dutch case (there are, for instance, no visible indications of *Werk* divisions) and may reflect outside influence, notably French. Neither flats nor towers are divided in tier, and the vertical divisions are so slight as to give the main front the appearance of one continuous line of pipes. Unusual though not unique is the carved and painted wooden canopy (blue lined with red and with gold fringe and tassels) suspended over the whole, perhaps as an aid to acoustics. Musical putti decorate the main case, whose over-hang is supported on slender columns, as elsewhere in Holland (13,18, 20). The usual civic pride is reflected in the armorial bearings of various local worthies carved along the gallery and main case impost, and surmounting the *Positief*. Though the latter repeats the capping of the main central tower, its plan differs from that of the main case and it ends in a magnificent acanthus *cul-de-lampe*.

The nineteenth-century display pipes are lacquered in bronze.

HAARLEM   Sint-Bavokerk (Grote Kerk)
One of Holland's most famous instruments (1735–8), in this respect probably second only to   29
that at Alkmaar (13), and with a good claim also to be considered one of the most visually satisfying of all North European organs.

In planning the case the organ builder, Christiaan Müller of Amsterdam, worked in close co-operation with Hendrick de Werff (town architect of Haarlem), the painter Hendrick van Limborch, and the sculptors Jan van Logteren and Jan Baptist Xaverij. Between them they produced a case which, although repeating a number of features which could by this time be considered as conventional—for example, the figures of Music and Poetry on the *Positief*, and those of David and other musicians on the main case—manages somehow to infuse them with a new vigour and grace. Even the town coat-of-arms with its lion supports which forms the decorative apex has about it an inevitable logic which is very pleasing.

Much of the success of this case must be attributed to its proportions, which in this particular context are surely as nearly perfect as possible. A Gothic organ which had preceded Müller's instrument had been positioned on the north wall, according to ancient custom; when the new organ was built the west end window had to be bricked up to accommodate it. After recent restoration the main colour scheme of gilded pipe shades and other carvings contrasted with plain woodwork makes its full effect on the visitor.

TEEFFELEN   Sint-Benedictus
After the grandiose conceptions of the preceding plates it is refreshing to come across this   30
very small mid-eighteenth century instrument by an anonymous builder, especially designed for an equally small village church. Despite its miniature size, however, it has been designed and constructed with care and without skimping; the carving of the pipe shades and side-pieces is bold, that of the acanthus leaves and charming bunch of grapes beneath the towers crisp and convincing.

NIJKERK   Nederlandse Hervormde Kerk

31   Built 1756 by Matthijs van Deventer of Nijmegen. The unfortunate clock and the absence of pointed towers, indeed the general rounded effect of this case, seems to indicate South Netherlandish influence. The proportions of the *Positief* are perhaps over-broad as compared with the main case, and the amount and weight of carving (amongst which are some Rococo motifs) are somewhat indigestible. Not a visually happy creation.

'S-GRAVENHAGE   Morgensternkerk

32   Chamber organ of *c.* 1740, with single flat of display pipes set in a frame of swirling Rococo C-scrolls which can be concealed behind doors. This is the first example in this book of the specifically secular development of the original Renaissance positive organ, for although now housed in a church this (and most of the instruments like it) was undoubtedly intended for domestic use. From its earliest days the chamber organ looked, as it was meant to do, more like a piece of domestic furniture than an organ, and as time went on this deception extended to making such instruments look as much like desks, bureaux, bookcases and the like as possible. Many of them are by anonymous organ builders and cabinet-makers, although on the other hand some famous builders are almost as well known for their chamber organs as they are for their church instruments.

HELMOND   Sint-Lambertus

33   The non-Dutch appearance of this case is explained by the fact that it was originally built for Averbode abbey in Belgium by Guillaume Robustelly of Liège in 1771. It came to Helmond in 1822.

At Averbode the organ had to be built so as not to obscure the west window, which to some extent explains its width; such proportions, however, are in any event more typical of French and South Netherlands cases than the vertical character of Dutch examples. Also typical of the former is the emphasis placed upon the main end towers rather than on the central one. The carved fronds and vases represent the more restrained kind of French decoration of the period (looking back to Louis XIV), and the musical instruments on the main towers blend well, though they are of the nineteenth century. The putti on the end towers are from a pulpit.

SCHIEDAM   Stedelijk Museum

34   Built in 1773 by H. H. Hess of Gouda for the chapel of the Sint-Jacobsgasthuis which is now the Museum. A small case in which the central tower seems too large and the triple divisions of the flats too fussy. The Rococo carving has considerable charm, in particular the floral *cul-de-lampe* and the side trophies of musical instruments. The linear quality of the looped garland on the central tower (whose cap also seems too big) contains an element of Neo-classicism.

AMSTERDAM   Sint-Franciscus-van-Assisië

35   A pleasantly fluid Rococo case of *c.* 1775, especially notable for the unusual division of the central section into two distinct parts divided by an emphatic impost. The lower portion has the visual character of a *Positief* which has been incorporated within the main body of the case. The delicacy of the whole is notably enhanced by the shallow side-pieces with their trophies of musical instruments, by the musical putti, and by the charming vase and garland overtopping the composition.

LEIDERDORP   Nederlandse Hervormde Kerk

Built in 1781 by Johann Mittelreyter of Leiden on a simple U–U–U plan, subsequently 36
much copied in Holland until as late as the 1920s and '30s, and here given some slight
additional interest by the gentle incurving of the two flats. The decoration is a curious mixture
of late Rococo (in the naturalistic branches carved beneath the case and at the pipe feet) and
strong Neo-classicism as exemplified in the gigantic vases crowning the towers. A curious
feature of the overall effect is the *trompe l'oeil* drapery painted on the wall behind the case.

BOLSWARD   Martinikerk (Grote Kerk)

Built *c.* 1775 by Albert Anthoni Hinsz, who has here somewhat improved upon the general 37
design of his earlier organ at Zwolle (27), though still maintaining its basic plan. Hinsz
however, seems to have had an unfortunate talent for spoiling his work by the addition of
unsightly ornament. At Zwolle we find the ugly tower caps (admittedly squashed down for
lack of space), the welter of heavy carving and the ill-proportioned figure of David. Here at
Bolsward our attention to the excellent proportions of the case is fatally distracted by the
figures of David (once again) with musical children on the *Positief*, and by Neo-classical
figures and clusters of drums and trumpets on the main towers. These last are in fact reminiscent of nothing so much as the mechanical figures on a fairground organ. In this organ case
the old-style outlines fail conspicuously to blend with new-style ornament.

AMSTERDAM   Stichting Amstelhof

An early nineteenth-century chamber organ exemplifying all that is best in the tradition of 38
convincing concealment which is such a feature of these instruments. In cases of this type it
is usual to find that the keyboard and drawstops can also be hidden by one means or another,
in addition to the pipes and bellows; the illusion is then complete. Here the pyramidal arrangement of the drawstops is attractive and original. Part of the bellows can be seen hanging down
behind the false drawer front.

ELBURG   Nederlandse Hervormde Kerk

Built in 1825 by G. H. Quellhorst of Oldenzaal, who despite his German origins and though 39
building here in Holland has nevertheless provided a French-looking case. The decorative
elements are a curious and somewhat uncomfortable mixture of classicism (the side volutes
and pendant swags of the *Positief* and winged herms supporting the end towers of the main
case), the Rococo (the side-pieces of the main case and naturalistic top borders of the *Positief*
flats) and Neo-classicism (urns and central group of lyre, palms and book on the main case
towers). The *Positief* figures of David supported by Music and Poetry are by now entirely
traditional.

BOXTEL   Sint-Petrus

Built during the early nineteenth century by Franciscus C. Smits of Reek (North Brabant), 40
this case in its general appearance recalls the much earlier one at Dordrecht (15), although
here all the towers are rounded and the proportions of the *Positief* towers are reversed; there is,
however, the same arrangement of flats and towers leading to a central apex, the same high
level of the display front, and the same tall pedal towers at each end.

   As so often happens in later Dutch organs, the generally harmonious proportions of the
case are spoiled by the undoubtedly well-carved but unnecessarily top-heavy figures of
Faith, Hope and Charity and groups of drums and trumpets on top of the main case towers.

SCHIJNDEL   Sint-Serviatus

41   Another organ by Smits (1839), the case on this occasion designed in Gothic Revival style. An interesting and not unsuccessful attempt to recreate the spirit, if not the letter, of a medieval case by introducing such details as embossed pipes, Gothic tracery, carved figures of angels, and motifs borrowed from Gothic architecture.

However, the difference may readily be detected by comparing this case with those at Middelburg or the Rijksmuseum (1, 5). For example, Smits's case is rather over-decorated for its apparent period (presumably *c.* 1500), and the division of the central tower into two tiers was a later development. The whole flavour of the case is slightly 'wrong', but it is nevertheless an attractive *jeu d'esprit*.

NAARDEN   Sint-Vituskerk (Grote Kerk)

42   Built in 1862 by C. G. F. Witte of Utrecht, this case neatly though hideously summarises all that is worst in terms of mid-nineteenth-century Gothic. The rigid lines of its composition seem to reflect the brand of religious and moral thought then prevailing in Protestant northern Europe, while its decoration is a typically insensitive mixture of different elements from the whole spectrum of the Gothic period. Moreover, from a musical standpoint, it is no longer possible, by looking at the front, to deduce what the general specification of the instrument may be.

This is indeed a poor exchange for the practical value and many visual felicities of the traditional Dutch organ case, whose final knell it sounds. One is additionally saddened to learn that a genuine Gothic case of *c.* 1520 was removed to make way for it.

Netherlands (South)

TIENEN Sint-Germanus

Of doubtful authorship and date, though probably originally not later than *c.* 1520, and the 43
most ancient case extant in Belgium today. Since its original construction, however, many
changes have taken place in the appearance of the case, to say nothing of the instrument inside it.

In its general appearance one can see the ghost of the 1526 case in the Amsterdam Rijksmuseum (5), more especially in that the front is almost wholly flat, the only emphasis being
provided by the single central tower. This general aspect, together with the *Positief* case, is
probably about all that can safely be said to remain of the original instrument.

The organ's first restoration took place in 1642; on this occasion the original pipe shades
and other details including carved figures were removed. During the following period of just
under 250 years no fewer than eight different programmes of restoration and rebuilding took
place, ranging from minor repairs to quite extensive alterations, and it is reasonable to suppose
that some if not all of these affected the case in greater or lesser degree. The last and most
extensive programme was carried out in 1888–91 and involved moving the organ from a site
under the tower at the west end of the church to a new gallery in the main aisle, where the
Positief is said to protrude a good deal less than it did before the move. (Most probably the
organ began its life on the north wall and was moved at a later date to the west end, perhaps
in 1642.) The occasion was also taken to add a figure of St Gregory to the *Positief* and to
'restore' the face of the main case according to nineteenth-century ideas of Gothic. As a
result perhaps the only really original Gothic detail remaining is a carving beneath the
central tower of a local hobgoblin known as the 'Grietmuil', a scourge of drunkards; this is
in the same tradition of medieval humour in carving that gave Western Europe its miseri-
cords and gargoyles.

QUENAST Saint-Martin

Although the church dates only from 1855 the organ came to it from Liège (either Saint- 44
Barthélemy or Saint-Martin), and was originally built in 1540 by Jan Verrydt. Five years
earlier he had built an organ at Tongerlo with a notable case carved by Hendrik Kools, and
it is probable that the same carver was employed here also. The ornament is pre-eminently
Renaissance in style, notably in the panels of wreathed three-dimensional heads that were a
popular feature of the style both in furniture and in decoration. (In England their appearance
in terracotta on the walls of Hampton Court Palace was one of the earliest manifestations of
the tardy arrival of Renaissance influence on the visual arts.) We have already encountered
them at Middelburg (2, 3) and Enkhuizen (8).

This case is perhaps the earliest extant example of the so-called 'Liège' type, in which the
single central U-tower forms the apex of a stepped composition, and in which the outermost
flats are slightly convex (see also 17). Here the generally flowing lines of the whole are
beautifully underscored by the curved brackets supporting the overhang at each side.

LIÈGE   Saint-Denis

45   Completed in 1589 (dated on the facetted vaulting beneath the *Positief*), the organ was the work of Nicolaes Niehoff, whose cabinet-maker on this and perhaps other occasions was Jan Schalken. Nicolaes was the son of Hendrik Niehoff (see plates 8–10), and may be said here to have translated his father's conception of a vertically-planned case, its front subdivided into a number of different areas, into terms of a broader, three-towered front which is much more simply divided. The most marked similarity between this case and those of the elder Niehoff at Enkhuizen and Abcoude is the somewhat compressed appearance of the *Positief* front. A similar case by Nicolaes Niehoff in the church of St Gereon in Cologne was unfortunately destroyed during the Second World War.

The decoration of the case is predominantly Renaissance, though verging on the Baroque, especially in the flamboyant pipe shades and the crowning of the intervening flats (unless, indeed, these are eighteenth-century in origin). The original shutters, painted by Philippe Libermé, have been lost, and the unsightly box-like features on the main tower tops surely cannot be original; most probably they replaced lantern turrets or figures similar to those of the three saints in the *Positief* (the central one being St Denis himself). Some restoration of the case took place in 1717, and in 1815–16 the height of the towers is said to have been slightly increased. The *Positief* case is now empty.

LIÈGE   Saint-Jacques

46   Dated 1600, the work of an anonymous builder, and so far as is known not significantly altered in appearance since then. The general design of the main front is in the 'Liège' tradition, and the decoration is textbook High Renaissance, the open lantern crowns being especially representative of the style and period.

The original polychrome colouring has been lost, as have also the painted shutters. These details apart, the case is a particularly fine example of its period and moreover is relatively unspoiled.

LIER   Sint-Gummarus

47   A travelled case, built 1628 to replace a Gothic organ (using much of the latter's pipework), removed in 1861 to a church at Nieuwmoer, bought back for Sint-Gummarus in 1929 and finally reinstalled there after the Second World War, though in a different position (i.e. above the west door).

This case, mainly in spirited though controlled Baroque style, is the work of François Peris, primarily a sculptor, with assistance in carving from Nicolaes Boullin. The proportions are especially pleasing, and there is a carefully-judged ratio of extraneous decoration as against display flats. The blind lantern turrets are a legacy from the Renaissance, and in fact, although the decoration is primarily early Baroque in style, there are other backward glances to the Renaissance, notably in the ornament of the gallery parapet and in the three panels below the main case impost. Both cases are spoiled at present by the lack of proper display pipes.

WATERVLIET   Onze-Lieve-Vrouw-Hemelvaart

48   A case of the 'Liège' type (though with V-shaped end towers), designed and built 1643–6 by the Bruges organ builder Baudewyn Le Dou and probably carved by Jacques Desy. Main and *Positief* cases should be regarded as an entity with the entrance screen and gallery above, carved by Jacques Sauvage, Christiaen Malieu and Pieter de Puttere and completed in 1649.

Though of late date the decoration of this whole area is Renaissance in style rather than Baroque, the nearest approach to the latter being the profile seraphs forming the side-pieces (a characteristic of Flemish cases). Over the central main tower rises a *Kroonwerk* containing display pipes, and the proportions of the case were spoiled *c*. 1750 by the addition above this of an ugly-looking clock framed in a cartouche, and by the removal, at the same time, of four carved figures whose pedestals still remain. Despite this, the conception as a whole is an impressive and mainly successful one.

LISSEWEGE   Onze-Lieve-Vrouw

A case stepped in the 'Liège' manner, though again with V-shaped end towers. The influence   49
of Liège can clearly be seen by making a comparison with the case at Quenast (44).

The case was carved in 1653–4 by Walram Rombouts to house an instrument by Baudewyn Le Dou. Rombouts's work here is richly Baroque, though elements of the Renaissance still linger (cf. 48).

GENT   Sint-Baafskathedraal

Built 1653–6 by Pierre Destrée and Louis Bys of Lille, with case by the woodcarver Jacques   50
Sauvage of Gent. French influence (presumably via Destrée and Bys) is apparent in the rounded towers and disposition of the flats, but the carving is an exuberant though typically lumpy Flemish interpretation of late Italian Renaissance ornament; it is not yet Baroque. The plate shows the main case, facing west above the entrace to the north ambulatory; the *Positief* case faces east. In 1819 the addition of a 32-foot stop necessitated the raising of the two trumpeting angels on pedestals and some alteration to the *Kroonwerk*, which in any event does not fit very well into the general design.

ANTWERP   Sint-Paulus

An important and influential instrument built by Nicolaes van Haeghen in 1648–54 into a   51
case designed by the artist Erasmus Quellin II and carved by Pieter Verbrugghen I.

The close similarity to the case of van Haeghen's organ at Dordrecht (15) is notable. The supposition is that the Antwerp case, being the earlier by some seventeen years, was used as the model. The pedal towers were not added here until 1732 (by J.-B. Forceville); it is therefore conceivable that the Dordrecht towers are also later additions. In both cases the final front plan emerges as U–V–U–V–U, with the innermost flats in tiers.

The overlarge angels, with crouching dragons at their feet, were added with the pedal towers, as was additional carved decoration, though not the charming *Positief* putti which are original. The crowning phoenix eventually became symbolically and cruelly ironic, for during the night of April 2/3, 1968, much damage was done to the organ in a fire which swept through the church.

MECHLIN   Onze-Lieve-Vrouw-over-de-Dijle

Built 1665–9 by Jan Bremser, the case carved 1667–9 by Jan Vergaelen, who thought so   52
highly of his own work here that he requested, and was eventually granted, burial at its foot. It is placed above the choir entrance, and was already the third organ to be built for the church.

The main case, of which the *Positief* is a replica in miniature, is well-proportioned, and although the carving is rich it is mostly not excessive; the figures of St Cecilia with attendant musical cherubs are especially pleasing. Unfortunately one cannot say the same for those of the Virgin and Child which, together with angels, large scallop shell and the pediment on which they all rest, give the impression (rightly or wrongly) of having been added during a rebuild which took place in 1842.

SAINT-HUBERT   Basilique Saint-Hubert

Built in 1685 by Antoine Picard, the sculptor/carver remaining unknown. The truncating of   53 the central main tower deprives the front of an emphasis which is not compensated for by the weak eighteenth-century heraldic and other additions inserted between the outer towers. Nor is the *tout ensemble* enhanced by the uncased modern pipes which flank it. However, this is amply offset by the wealth of fine Baroque carving with which both the *Positief* and main case are covered. It is noticeable that the proportion of woodwork to display pipes is much higher in the *Positief* than in the main case.

STALHILLE   Sint-Jan-Baptist

54   A small case of great charm housing an instrument made in 1715 by Jacobus van Eynde of Ypres; previously in Bruges before installation at Stalhille in 1785. The sculptor is unknown, though Jan van der Plancke has been suggested (see 55). The style of the case recalls that at Lier (47) and to a lesser extent—though not in the 'Liège' form—those at Watervliet and Lissewege (48, 49). This case is designed to be free-standing and has perforated panels at the rear to let the sound out.

The carving is masterly throughout, although one is especially attracted to the naturalistic fruit-and-flowers *cul-de-lampe* beneath the central tower and the baskets of the same on top of all three towers. The carved angels too are full of life and vigour; it is noticeable that they play good representations of cornetts (as opposed to the vague and inaccurate paintings and carvings of musical instruments all too often found on organ cases). The strongly nasal sound of the cornett (a six-sided wooden instrument, often covered in leather, with a cup-shaped mouthpiece) was basic to the wind band of the period, and was also imitated with some success in organ stops; indeed there could originally have been such a stop in this organ.

BRUGES   Sint-Salvatorkathedraal

55   Built 1717–19 in collaboration between the organ builder Jacobus van Eynde, Michiel Clauwert, cabinet-maker, and Jan van der Plancke, sculptor. It stood then on a marble screen of 1679–82 which divided choir from nave; the main case faced into the nave, the *Positief* into the choir. During a rebuild of 1936 both screen and organ were moved to the west wall of the church and the latter rearranged; at the same time the two pedal towers were designed in keeping and crowned with the figures of David and St Cecilia which had formerly been on the outer towers of the main case. Their places there were taken by the two string-playing putti which had formerly been on the *Positief*.

Despite the eighteenth-century date of the main case the general style (e.g., double-tiered central tower, triple-tiered flats) and some of the decoration suggests that either the design or actual parts of an older case were used. The panelled area below the main case impost is presumably eighteenth century. The carved side-pieces were originally those of the main case, suitably enlarged and transposed to the pedal towers in 1936.

ANTWERP   Sint-Carolus

56   After a serious fire in 1708 Jean-Baptiste Forceville was engaged to build a new organ in a case carved and probably also designed by Jan Pieter van Baurscheit I. The design, however, will have been provided in close consultation with Forceville, for the latter also built another organ similar not only in siting (in front of the west window) and general design but also in many details of the decoration, for the church of Sint-Pieter-en-Pauwel in Mechlin.

This case represents an attempt to incorporate what would normally be a separate *Positief* within the main front, while maintaining the clear visual separation of this part of the case from the rest; this section is housed in the central tower and two supporting flats. The result is a very wide case which might be more acceptable to the eye if the overhang at each end were not so great; as it is, it looks somewhat top-heavy and uncomfortable.

The general effect of the excellent carving is also spoiled by the fussy trophies of musical instruments below the impost. An unusual feature is the substitution of carved tasselled lappets which replace the more normal forms of pipe shade.

ANTWERP Sint-Jacob

Another instrument (1727–9) by J.-B. Forceville (cf. 56), whose *penchant* was for width rather than height in case design—indeed, he was the first organ builder to introduce wide as opposed to high cases in the South Netherlands. Here again, as in Sint-Carolus, the *Positief* is the connecting link between the two higher-placed halves of the *Groot Orgel*. However, in fairness to Forceville it should be said that this was a later idea; originally the space was to remain unfilled while *Groot Orgel* and *Pedaal* formed two separate cases. 57

The caving here is by Michiel van der Voort I, who also made the case. Given the strongly architectural character of this case one cannot help regarding the otherwise charming angels and musical putti as Rococo irrelevancies in this context.

TOURNAI Saint-Jacques

By Pierre-Joseph and Jean de Ryckere of Courtrai, 1753–5, cabinet-maker unknown. A French-style case in its general appearance and the arrangement of flats and towers. The Rococo pipe shades are not confined within a cornice, though the towers remain heavily capped. The carved panelling, putti and musical instrument trophies of the main case bespeak the Rococo elegance of the Régence period, while the simple grandeur of the display front is enhanced by the larger musical trophies that form the side-pieces. 58

The *Positief* is a miniature replica of the main case, while the gallery on which it sits is likewise carved with musical trophies and forms an entity with the organ as a whole.

TONGEREN Onze-Lieve-Vrouw

This thoroughly French-looking instrument was built *c.* 1750–3 by Jean-Baptiste le Picard of Liège and carved by Martin Termonia of the same city. 59

The front can in fact be regarded as a clever double repetition of the *Positief*, joined by a single low flat. One's pleasure in the harmonious proportions of the whole composition with its nicely-judged proportion of Rococo carving is somewhat spoiled by the superfluous group of Madonna and angels under a canopy, all of which seem to have been added as an afterthought; they surely cannot have been conceived as an integral part of the original design. Nor is one greatly attracted to the soup-tureen effect of the *Positief* tower caps, crowned by vases. The pipe shades here are reduced to the absolute minimum.

POPERINGE Onze-Lieve-Vrouw

Case *c.* 1760 by the local cabinet-maker Emmanuel Walwijn. In its general design his work here most recalls the case at Stalhille (54), though there the end towers are pointed and there is no *Positief*. It is noticeable that the *Positief* here at Poperinge makes no attempt to echo in any way the main case behind it except in general style. 60

The wide projection of the side-pieces is especially noticeable in this French-inspired case, while the carving, in its luxuriance and motifs, seems to point backward to the period of Louis XIV rather than forward to that of Louis XVI. The important contribution made by the gallery rail and its supporting acanthus frieze to the success of the composition as a whole is another notable feature here.

MECHLIN Sint-Jan

Case planned and perhaps partly executed by the sculptor Theodoor Verhaegen of Mechlin 61 in 1759, and completed after his death in that year by his pupil Pieter Valckx, who had completed the whole case by 1781. Much of the other woodwork in the church is also by these two masters. The instrument originally housed in the case was by Pieter van Peteghem I, a pupil of J.-B. Forceville.

The design of the case marks an entirely new departure in the way the whole composition rises to its apex in a graceful series of Rococo-inspired volute shapes, the habitual pre-eminence of the central tower being subordinated to the general design. With its usual unerring poor taste the nineteenth century has managed to spoil some of the effect by the addition of an unnecessary medallion (featuring King David) at the top. Apart from this it would be hard to find a case that more successfully expresses the essentially fluid nature of the Rococo style, though in so doing something of the character of the instrument itself is inevitably lost.

HARINGE   Sint-Martinus

62 An apparently unspoiled instrument by Pieter van Peteghem I and his son Lambertus Benôit, built 1778–9. Among the more rare of its stops are the *Rossignol*, which imitates the song of the nightingale by means of several small pipes standing in water, and the *Tambours*, pedal pipes mis-tuned to represent the noise of drums.

The case bears the date 1778 and the signature of the carver Jan Elshoecht, French-domiciled though born in Brussels. It is graceful and quietly competent, and the gallery parapet in particular, with its trophies of musical instruments, bears witness to the high quality of the carving. One feels, however, that it would have been better to omit the figures (David, Holy Church and St Cecilia), whose unfortunate drunken appearance is due to the shape of the wooden roof above them. It may be that the available roof space was found to be much less than had been supposed, but that it was felt preferable to include the figures in a leaning attitude rather than to omit them altogether.

BELSELE   Sint-Andries-en-Ghislanus

63 Another organ by Pieter I and Lambertus Benôit Peteghem, built 1784–5. The fine main case incorporates—from a previous seventeenth-century organ in the church—the two musical putti on the outer towers and two panels (not visible in the plate) also carved with musical angels and with drapery. Tasselled lappets are again used instead of pipe shades, as at Sint-Carolus, Antwerp (56), and the side-pieces of musical-instrument trophies are especially impressive.

The *Positief* case is a nineteenth-century addition but is not inharmonious with the total composition.

AVERBODE   Abdij (Abbey)

64 With this pseudo-Renaissance extravaganza the organ case in the South Netherlands, as in the North, finally ceases to reflect the character and technical composition of the instrument it houses, just as surely as the nature of the instrument itself is changed. The latter here was built 1853–61 by Hippolyte Loret, and the case was carved by A. Piersotte of Elsene. Apart from commending his obvious skill there is nothing else that can usefully be said about this case, except to remark on its resemblance to a gigantic *Kroonwerk* and on the paucity of its *Positief*.

Austria, Germany, Switzerland

SION (SW)   Notre-Dame-de-Valère

A basically ancient case dating at least from 1433 (when it is first mentioned in the church   65
records) and having the typical medieval flat front with painted wings. The latter date from
c. 1435 and have been attributed to Peter Maggenberg of Fribourg; they are of canvas
stretched on wooden frames and show the Annunciation (exterior), the Virgin and Child with
St Catherine (interior, left) and Christ's post-Resurrection appearance to St Mary Magdalene
(interior, right). The exterior canvases have been removed and put under glass elsewhere in
the church. The case itself is also painted in polychrome.

The builder of both case and instrument is unknown, though the organ has been compared
to the work of Henri Arnaut of Zwolle. It was rebuilt in 1718 but still contains a number of
original medieval pipes. Situated in a 'swallow's nest' at the back of the church, it recalls the
miniature castles of medieval illuminated manuscripts. Of the two crenellated towers, the
left-hand one is slightly broader than the other; it is noticeable that their openwork pipe
shades do not match, while that from the central flat is presumably missing. The frieze above
the impost dates only from 1954, having been put in as part of a scheme of restoration carried
out in that year, but it is perfectly suited to the rest of the case.

It is to be regretted that the silhouette of this ancient case has to some extent been spoiled
by the addition in 1718 of the pedal pipes behind it.

It is interesting to note that the design of the case is very closely paralleled by that of a
positive organ illustrated in *Spiegel der Orgelmacher und Organisten,* a rare work published in
1511 by the blind German organist Arnold Schlick of Mainz. The only significant visual differences between Schlick's positive and the organ at Sion are that the former has no wings and is
smaller in overall size. This marked similarity is a further indication of the close links between
the positive and the evolving church organ during the late Gothic and Renaissance periods.

KIEDRICH (G)   Sankt Valentin

A basically medieval organ of about 1495 which, however, owes its impressive and con-   66
vincing appearance to a scholarly nineteenth-century restoration. This was carried out under
the supervision of the English antiquary and organ enthusiast, Sir John Sutton, who first
visited Kiedrich in 1857 and restored the organ in 1858–60 at his own expense. Sutton, a
Gothic Revival enthusiast of note and friend of A. W. N. Pugin, was advised here by a fellow
Englishman, the Rev. John Gibson, whose interests and abilities were similar to his own.
Under their guidance much of the casework was renewed and new carving provided; mean-
while a late seventeenth-century *Positiv* and a gallery of 1760 were removed and a 'swallow's
nest' gallery (designed by Gibson) introduced instead. The whole composition of the organ
in its gallery was now made to stand out against a simulated painted carpet held by trumpeting
angels. This was probably painted by August Martin, who also painted the shutters with
scenes from the Nativity and Epiphany.

The Kiedrich case is an example of the Gothic Revival at its best.

LÜBECK (G)   Sankt Jakobi

67   This is the smaller of the two famous organs in Sankt Jakobi, both of which miraculously escaped the damage inflicted on most of the other organs in the city during the Second World War. It is situated in the north aisle and is thought to date from about 1500, though it is possible that the central part is even older, pre-1490, the two outer towers having been added at a slightly later date. The *Positiv* dates from 1637, and was provided by the organ builder Friedrich Stellwagen; this is obviously of a more Baroque cast than the main case, and in the self-confident manner of the time bears at its apex the heraldic arms and name of the local merchant who donated it. The upper tiers of pipes in the *Positiv* are not original.

In 1890 the original colouring of the main case was restored as far as possible. At the same time the opportunity was taken of painting faces round the mouths of the display pipes on both the main and *Positiv* cases, in imitation of the Renaissance grotesque style. The tongues of flame carved between the feet of the display pipes on the main case are a Baroque feature and therefore probably date from the seventeenth century (see also 11, 73, 112, 116).

INNSBRUCK (A)   Silberne Kapelle

68   A famous Italian-built positive of *c.* 1550, notable for the fact that all its front pipes, as well as many inside, are of wood. The use of predominantly wooden pipes was customarily reserved —in Renaissance Italy—for chamber organs, but this is the only important example to have survived. It is possibly identical with a wooden-pipe organ that was presented in 1571 to Archduke Ferdinand II of Tyrol by an Italian organ builder, Marcario Ceralto di Spello, who was then working in Trent. The case front is a compressed version of a typical Italian design, the decoration richly High Renaissance in character.

AUGSBURG (G)   Sankt Anna, Fuggerkapelle

69   This is a fine reconstruction (1957) of the original 1512 case which was destroyed through war damage in 1944. Its design has sometimes been attributed to the painter Hans Burgkmair, and is especially remarkable for two things: (a) it is designed in relation to the circular window behind, and (b) in the absence of pipe shades, the totally flat front, the arrangement of display pipes and the employment of round-headed pipe compartments it is clearly influenced by Italian ideas. Burgkmair visited Italy as a young man, and the merchant banking Fugger family (whose chapel this is) had many business connections with that country. It is not surprising, therefore, that the style and decoration of this case should reflect so strongly the tremendous impact of the Italian Renaissance.

The visual connections of this organ with religion are of the slightest and, one feels, the most perfunctory; indeed they extend only to the larger pair of wings, happily preserved, and painted by Jörg Breu I in 1517–22 with scenes of the Ascension and Assumption. The wings of the rigidly-framed *Positiv*, on the other hand, also painted by Breu, show Pythagorus making musical experiments (left) and the court choir of the Emperor Maximilian; when closed they show an allegory of the invention of music. Though gratifying to musicians, the inspiration behind this painting and indeed behind the case as a whole is clearly secular and humanist, not religious, and as such is an excellent illustration of Renaissance philosophy.

KONSTANZ (G)   Münster

70   Gallery and organ were built together in 1516–20, builder unknown. The most striking features of this case are the *trompe l'œil* painted panels connecting the upper tier of the central section with the two outermost compartments. Although the illusion of perspective is instantly destroyed when the eye recognises the straight line of the impost, it is probably more successful when seen from ground level.

The carving of the impost, pipe shades (the central three dated 1518) and dividing verticals of the tripartite central section is lively and vigorous, as is also that of the angel trumpeters in front of the gallery. A *Positiv* added probably in the seventeenth century was sensibly removed during a rebuild in 1853. However, at the same time—less sensibly—the original substructure of the case was removed and the decorated display pipes were melted down and re-formed into the present ones. The original shutters painted by Matheus Gutrecht II were removed (though parts of them have been preserved) and the whole case was painted over in a uniform buff colour.

In 1922–3 the case was cleaned, repainted and regilded in its original colouring. In 1954–5, as part of a rebuilding scheme, it was moved further back on the gallery and the lower part boarded up in a very ugly and inappropriate manner.

NÖRDLINGEN (G)   Sankt Georg

The basic outline of this case may be that of a 1466 organ built by Stephen Castendorfer (or   71
Kaschendorff), though the two small sections next to the outer towers are certainly later additions; they spoil the proportions width-wise, their pipe shades are not confined within a cornice and are in a different style of decoration.

None of the pipe shades in fact date from 1466, the main ones probably being from a rebuild of 1544–6 by Benedikt Klotz of Dinkelsbühl; some carving was done at this time by the sculptor Hans Fuchs and painting (including perhaps the musicians on the brackets) by Jesse Herlin. From this period also may come the distinctive 'lace curtain' pipe shades of the *Brustwerk*.

Between 1605 and 1610 further alterations and additions took place, including the painting of the wings and gallery panels by Johann Simon Metzger. The awkward projecting of the left-hand shutter, due to the organ's position on a gallery in the south aisle, makes one doubt that this was in fact its original situation; certainly there seems to have been a period when it was moved to the west end, i.e. from the mid-seventeenth to the nineteenth centuries. The modern display pipes would have looked more authentic if their mouths had been arranged in a straight line according to Gothic practice.

KLOSTERNEUBURG (A)   Stiftskirche

This case was reconstructed in 1642 (date on a small cartouche just above the *Brustwerk*)   72
from an earlier one in the church, to house an instrument built by Johann Georg Freundt of Passau which mostly still exists and which also utilised pipes from an earlier organ. The instrument itself is the only work of Freundt still extant, as well as being the largest extant organ of its period in Austria.

The case shows little evidence of earlier work, unless its general outline be compared with that at Nördlingen (71). The mixture of single- and double-tier flats strikes a slightly discordant note, and the design of the *Positiv* is considerably more fluid than that of the main case, although its decoration—especially the *culs-de-lampe* and the lozenge-like shapes at the pipe feet—seems to belong rather to the Renaissance than to the Baroque. The carved figures are a welcome change from the usual ones of David, St Cecilia and the like; here they represent three of the Four Latin Fathers of the Church, SS. Ambrose, Augustine and Gregory (on top of the main towers), plus St Nicholas and the first provost of Klosterneuburg (flanking the *Brustwerk*). The original three pairs of wings have now vanished.

Two other points remain to be noticed. First, is the crowning of the central *Positiv* tower perhaps a relic of the earlier Gothic organ? Secondly, the pipe shades do not mask the tops of the display pipes but follow their outline in a series of steps, even though this means that the shades themselves are irregularly balanced.

STADE (G)   Sankt Cosmae-et-Damiani

73   This type of case—broad but low, on the plan U–V–U–V–U, the continuous cornice only broken significantly by the central tower, the flats partly or wholly in tier—is especially characteristic of North Germany and is stylistically linked also to organs in the North Netherlands (not surprisingly, since the builders were itinerant within the whole area). It is known as the 'Hamburg front' and is associated above all with the name of Arp Schnitger. Another constant feature of the design is the manner in which the pedal towers go well down below the impost.

The organ here at Stade was built 1669–73 by Berendt Huess of Glückstadt, but he was assisted by Schnitger, who was his cousin and later made certain modifications to the instrument. However, the original appearance of the organ was drastically altered by the enlargement of the gallery, probably in 1864, when the original *Positiv* was removed. It was reconstructed in 1949 as part of a general scheme of restoration, but looks thoroughly forlorn and lost without the support of the gallery parapet, a fact which once again emphasises the importance of the latter to the success of this type of composition.

Inverted shades round the pipe feet are a feature of this type of design and of those related to it.

CORVEY (G)   Klosterkirche

74   A case of similar type to the preceding, though less broad and more highly ornamented. There is a clear decorative unity between the case, the gallery and the realistic and almost life-size angels that support it. Flamboyant realism allied to illusionism is one of the more obvious hallmarks of the German Baroque style, of which this case is a good example. Here, as so often in cases of the type, it is most evident in the figures of the angels—not only those supporting the gallery but also the two musical ones perched on the side-pieces—the enchanting instrument-playing putti, and the seraphs whose wings and three-dimensional heads form the pipe shades.

The instrument was built by Andreas Schneider of Höxter in 1681 and the carving is attributed to Johann Sasse who did other work in the same church. The organ has no *Positiv*; this enables the viewer to see the console flanked by carved openwork panels and with two small flats of *Brustwerk* pipes above those panels.

NEUENFELDE (G)   Sankt Pankratii

75   Another 'Hamburg front', this time the unaided work of the great Arp Schnitger, who lies buried here. He settled at Neuenfelde in 1679 and married, as his second wife, a local girl whose father's farm he inherited. He himself presented the organ to the church, and his family crest can be seen above the altar.

The organ dates from 1688 and is a fine visual and tonal expression of Schnitger's work. The case shows how the organ at Stade (73) no doubt looked originally before the unfortunate broadening of the gallery, with the pedal towers actually forming a part of the gallery and their sides enclosing the keyboard area. The *Positiv* is a faithful replica of the central main case. (This is in fact a two-storey gallery, fairly common in this part of Germany.) The marbling of the case is an expression of the Baroque love for illusionism, for simulating marble and stone in wood, textiles (such as curtains and hangings) in marble, and so on.

LANDSHUT (G)   Sankt Martin

76   An odd-looking case whose origins seem to go back beyond the date 1700 lettered above the first tier of the central section. Most probably it is a hybrid (the two end sections were added in 1914). Though most of the display pipes are modern there are several old embossed

ones in the *Oberwerk* (below the clock) and some thirty original plain ones in the *Hauptwerk* (below the *Oberwerk*); the latter are upside down, having perhaps been placed thus as a substitute for the more usual pipe shades.

The rigid design of this case, together with the clock, is more reminiscent of a chimney-piece than an organ.

SANKT URBAN (SW)   Klosterkirche

During the Baroque and Rococo eras of the eighteenth century, and especially in South   77
Germany, Austria, and the adjoining parts of Switzerland, we meet for the first time the concept of moulding the organ case into the architectural setting of the building in which it is housed, so as to integrate it within the total design of the building. This often means that the case is designed round the window or windows of the west end (its usual situation in the church). So it is here at Sankt Urban. The date is 1716–21, the builder Joseph Bossart of Baar (Canton Zug), who also worked in the southern part of the Württemberg area.

The front plan is extremely diverse and fluid, and the style of flats and towers (especially the latter) quite new. It is no longer easy for the eye to pick out the tonal divisions of the organ—to recognise, for example, that the pedal pipes are housed in the two tall 'towers' and the pavilion-like sections above the open arches, or that the pipes in the novel three-cross arrangement at the apex (in fact part of the abbot's coat-of-arms) are those of the *Oberwerk*.

The lively carved decoration is Baroque, though hovering on the threshold of the Rococo; so too are the lifelike angels, the supporting Atlases, and King David, who in his presence and situation here is reminiscent of several Dutch organs. As at Klosterneuburg (72) the stepped pipe shades exactly follow the line of the pipe tops and so are not equal, though the inequalities are not so evident to the eye as they are at Klosterneuburg.

INNSBRUCK (A)   Sankt Jakob

Built 1725 by Johann Caspar Humpel of Merano, this organ (whose original pipes and   78
mechanism were removed in 1931) replaced the previous instrument destroyed with the church in an earthquake. The case is untypical and puzzling. In its general appearance and design the display front above the substructure recalls the mid-sixteenth-century cases at Freiburg (Germany) and the Hofkirche at Innsbruck; these were the work of Jörg Ebert of Ravensburg, who is known to have worked also in Sankt Jakob in 1566. Humpel's case may therefore reflect the general appearance of the original pre-earthquake case.

The decoration, however, is a different matter. It too is not typical of 1725 and suggests rather the Baroque style of approximately a century earlier. The carving of figures, side-pieces and pipe shades is correspondingly luxuriant, and the architectural perspective of the central section, achieved here by the clever arrangement of the pipes, is typical also of much cabinet furniture of the period 1600–25. The donor's arms over the same section are given characteristically florid Baroque treatment.

Two further points may be briefly noted (a) the absurdly small size of the *Positiv* in relation to the rest of the case; (b) the fact that the displayed pedal pipes in the two end compartments correspond in number but not in disposition to the steps of the pipe shades.

An unhappy and unsatisfactory case.

OCHSENHAUSEN (G)   Klosterkirche

Built 1729–33 by Joseph Gabler of Ochsenhausen (who trained originally as a cabinet-maker   79
before taking up organ building), and his first work. In *c.* 1750 Gabler combined the original four separate keyboards into a single three-manual raised console in the window-space, following the outline of the *Positiv*.

The fluid outlines and airy grace of this case reflect the spirit of the late Baroque, most marked perhaps in the antics of the smaller, almost doll-like putti. Less obvious though even more typical of the age is a mechanical toy consisting of a model ox housed on top of the *Positiv*; on being activated this emerges like a cuckoo from a clock, representing a play on the name Ochsenhausen.

Notice the way in which the two small display panels at the ends of the case spill over into the window embrasures. This case is more clearly moulded by and to its architectural setting than that at Sankt Urban (77), though less so than some later examples (83, 92).

BORGENTREICH (G)   Sankt Johannis Baptist

80 Originally built 1730–5 in the Klosterkirche at Dahlem by Johann Patroclus Möller of Lippstadt; brought to Borgentreich in 1803, dismantled in 1831, rebuilt in a different form in 1836, and rearranged yet again in 1951–2.

After so many changes it is impossible to say how closely the organ still resembles Möller's original conception; most probably it looked more like his organ at Marienfeld (87). The original *Positiv* was removed in 1836 and the present one is a reconstruction from 1952.

SANKT PETER (G)   Klosterkirche

81 An impressive 'window' case designed and decorated in the Baroque style perhaps by Johann Christian Wenzinger of Freiburg, architect and sculptor; it originally contained an instrument built 1732 by Johann Georg Fischer. St Cecilia and King David return to the scene once again.

The *Positiv* case, which may also be by Wenzinger, is of a later date and is in Rococo style, identifiable by the fluid composition formed at its base by the C-scroll shapes so typical of the style. The clock too is probably also of this period, the putti being cousins to those on the *Positiv*.

MELK (A)   Stiftskirche

82 For this famous monastery church the organ builder Gottfried Sonnholz of Vienna completed in 1732 an instrument divided into two entirely separate cases, with a *Positiv* as the connecting visual link between them.

The two parts of the main case consist almost entirely of towers, but very narrow flats containing a selection of correspondingly small pipes can be seen between them. The carved decoration of the actual cases is comparatively restrained for so rich an interior and is mainly confined to the pipe shades. On the other hand one gets the impression that the towers have been designed primarily as resting places for the angels and putti that perch upon them like so many roosting starlings.

WEINGARTEN (G)   Klosterkirche

83–5 This magnificent organ, the *chef d'œuvre* of Joseph Gabler (see also plate 79) was in building from 1737 to 1750. It is perhaps the supreme example of a case governed by architectural rather than tonal concepts, an approach which leads to immense technical complexities when it comes to devising the mechanisms which must link pipes to keyboard (here, as at Ochsenhausen, an early example of the detached console, situated under the central arch).

Possibly the case might not have been quite so extravagant had not Gabler been trained originally as a cabinet-maker. It was made on the monastery premises, decorated by one of the monks, and bears figures of angels and Atlases carved by the sculptor Joachim Früholz. It is interesting to note that without the two end towers the appearance of the organ would be very much more squat.

The organ was and still remains a muscial as well as a visual *tour de force*. Among its more unusual effects are stops for Cuckoo, Drum Nightingale, and two Carillons. The bells for the pedal Carillon are hung in imitation of grape clusters (a pun on the name 'Weingarten') and can be seen in plate 83 hanging in three 'bunches' beneath the central arch.

The pipe shades of the main case are in the form of looped curtains, a typical Baroque touch.

ROTTENBUCH (G) Mariä-Geburt-Kirche
A delicious confection in a setting of Rococo swirls, this organ was built in 1747 by Balthasar   86
Freiwiss of Aitrang. Here, as at Weingarten, one wonders at the mechanical skill and imagi-
native genius which enabled Freiwiss to construct his *Kronwerk* as a totally detached element
perched on a semicircular bridge (the whole section being reminiscent of the modern organ in
Llandaff cathedral, Wales).

Paintings incorporated into the substructure are vestigial reminders of the old painted
wings of Gothic and Renaissance cases. Pipe shades are formed of a mixture of carved drapery
and tasselled lappets; the latter also depend from the *Kronwerk*. The side-pieces, though still
present, are greatly reduced in size and are formed from Rococo scroll shapes instead of the
more usual trophies of musical instruments. The *Positiv* too is less assertive; it no longer
hangs from the gallery but is set flush with the parapet. The asymmetrical character of the
Rococo style is summed up in the decorative crowning of the central tower with its perching
cherub.

This is the first organ case in this book to express so clearly and completely the spirit and
style of the Rococo.

MARIENFELD (G) Klosterkirche
Built 1751 by Johann Patroclus Möller, this fine case seems to have been inspired by   87
the 'Hamburg' type. The main case, however, is very much more compact—so much so,
indeed, that the central section gives the impression of having been forcibly squeezed
together to produce the stepped effect. In contrast the *Positiv* is greatly extended. Another
variant is that the pedal towers are joined to the main case by concave flats.

EINSIEDELN (SW) Klosterkirche
Here we see the Epistle-side case of the divided *Chororgel*, situated in the retrochoir behind the   88
main sanctuary. The two cases are almost identical, except that the Epistle organ contains the
console and pedalboard. The builder (1751-4) was Viktor Ferdinand Bossart of Baar (Canton
Zug).

Despite its late date this case is more Baroque than Rococo, but as in many other examples
of the period the immediate attention of the viewer is almost wholly occupied by the antics
of the various attendant angels and putti.

ESSLINGEN (G) Sankt Dionysius
Built 1706 by Georg Allgeyer of Hofen. A divided case whose mainly straight lines empha-   89
sise the angular setting of plain walls, flat roof and simple west window. On the other hand
the carved and pierced pipe shades and crestings with their armorial bearings have a quiet
richness. The carved device of the Trinity symbol under a canopy surmounted by the figure
of David, which acts as a bridge between the two cases, is perhaps not entirely happy but
may have been added during a rebuild of 1752-4.

IRSEE (G) Klosterkirche
Built in 1754 on the architectural principles of Gabler by Balthasar Freiwiss. The decorations   90
of the case are not sufficiently asymmetrical to be considered as typically Rococo. The

provision of the detached console on a secondary gallery is unusual for this period. In the *Positiv* the shape of the west window is neatly echoed by the little central tower, while the two supporting towers are mirror images of those on the main case.

DIE WIES (G)   Wallfahrtskirche

91   The instrument was built *c.* 1756–9 by Andreas Jäger of Füssen, but it is inconceivable that he should have designed the case without reference to the architect Dominikus Zimmermann, whose pilgrimage church here is in every detail a masterpiece of the Rococo style. Most probably, in fact, Zimmermann designed this case himself; at all events it is a little jewel in its own right, though the actual front plan of the main case is surprisingly traditional. Here it is the *Positiv*, not the main case, which is divided and integrated into the parapet of the gallery (enhanced in the centre with typical Rococo openwork lattice), each half reversing the plan of the main case.

OTTOBEUREN (G)   Klosterkirche

92–4   Few organ cases can have been so successfully designed as integral parts of the surrounding architecture and decoration as the two identical ones which grace the choir of the Benedictine monastery at Ottobeuren. Completed in 1764, they are the only surviving work in this style of Karl Joseph Riepp (French-trained though a native of Ottobeuren), in consultation with the cabinet-maker Martin Hörmann and the sculptor Joseph Christian, and have been carefully planned so as to grow, apparently naturally, from the Rococo choir stalls below—in fact the whole church is a hymn of praise to the Rococo style, to which the organ cases are no exception.

In each organ the two smaller cases on the screen contain the *Positiv*. The main case consists of the tower, also rising from the screen, and two fronts placed at right angles to it and on each side of the pillar from which springs the arch. Behind the choir screen each of these fronts is found to stand on a gallery and over an arch beneath which is the console (94). This is a unique arrangement, and indeed the organs themselves are a tribute to the imaginative powers and technical skill of a unique genius. They are named respectively the Trinity organ (Epistle side), which has four manuals, and the Holy Ghost organ (Gospel side), which has two.

ROGGENBURG (G)   Stiftskirche

95   A fine pyramid-like Rococo case, built originally to house an instrument of 1752–61 by Georg Friedrich Schmahl of Ulm. The disengaged pillars standing proud of the front are an unusual feature. The over-small *Positiv* is dwarfed by the main case, and two sections of display pipes are missing.

ARLESHEIM (SW)   Dom

96   A very conservative-looking instrument for its period (1759–61), and thoroughly French in its case design. Both these points can be explained by the fact that the builder was Johann Andreas Silbermann of Strasbourg, who has here obviously followed the example of his father Andreas in his 1732 organ at Ébersmunster (145). This case at Arlesheim pays only restricted lip-service to the Rococo style in some of its decorative details, chiefly the side-pieces of both main and *Positiv* cases, and the cherub and other supports of the towers.

FISCHINGEN (SW)   Klosterkirche

97   Built 1763 by Johann Georg Aichgasser of Überlingen in Swabia. The ungainly width of this otherwise charming Rococo case is due to the fact that the end sections which contain the pedal pipes were added somewhat as an afterthought.

The cheerful marbling (in light blue and salmon pink!) gives a toy-like aspect to the whole composition.

ETTAL (G)   Klosterkirche
Built 1763 by Johann Georg Hörterich of Dirlewang. A thoroughgoing Rococo creation   98
which, though looking back to much earlier designs in the small two-tiered V-shaped towers
flanking the central section, in general recalls the design of the organ at Roggenburg (95).

BREGENZ (A)   Sankt Gallus
The last work of Joseph Gabler, who died in 1771 whilst actually working on it. In form this   99
is a far more conservative case than either Ochsenhausen (79) or Weingarten (83–85), almost
the only similarity to these being the pipe shades as at Ochsenhausen and the carved infilling
between the pipe feet (both organs). The substructure is surprisingly tall, forcing the display
front up to the low roof and pressing the *Kronwerk* down between the outer towers, instead of
letting it ride triumphantly over the whole. The Rococo decoration of the main case is likewise very restrained, although that of the *Positiv* is slightly more obvious.

HILZINGEN (G)   Sankt Peter-und-Paul
Built *c.* 1770, perhaps by a follower of Gabler. An attempt to reintroduce the old form of   100
towers with heavy caps—but the whole shape of the case is hidden beneath such a welter of
Rococo carving as to be almost indistinguishable at first sight. Except for those in the
Kronwerk, the display pipes, which date from a rebuild of 1960, do not reach up behind the
pipe shades and to this extent make nonsense of the general design.

SALEM (G)   Klosterkirche
It seems almost incredible that this case should originally have housed an instrument built   101
1770–3 by Riepp, for it bears no outward resemblance whatever to his masterpiece at
Ottobeuren (92–94). Called the Trinity organ and situated at the west end, it is the only
surviving one of the three organs which Riepp provided for the church. The design is
basically French (Riepp being based at Dijon), and so indeed is the decoration which is Neo-
classical, though the perching angels on the towers remain defiantly Baroque. The ornamentation of the case was carried out by Joseph Anton Feichtmayer and Johann Georg Dürr.

    A departure from French case design and continuance of the South German tradition is the
existence of the *Kronwerk* as a separate entity; in a totally French design this tonal department
is known as the *Écho* and is normally built into the main case.

STEINGADEN (G)   Klosterkirche
Built anonymously in 1743, this organ forms the main item in a wholly Rococo scheme of   102
decoration at the west end of the church. The actual arrangement of flats and towers remains
fairly conventional; it is the flowing outlines and characteristic decoration which impart the
full Rococo flavour. A notable feature of the overall design is the fluid architectural counter-
point formed by the outlines of the main case as opposed to those of the west window behind
it.

AMORBACH (G)   Abteikirche
The masterpiece of Johann Philipp and Johann Heinrich Stumm of Rhaunen-Sulzbach, built   103
1774–82; casework by Johannes Reinhard, carving by the brothers Jörg and Franz Ignatius
Schäffer. A wide, French-looking case, the decorative inspiration of the Rococo being less
immediately obvious than in many other examples, until we notice the relief trophies of

musical instruments below the impost, the swags of naturalistic flowers between the tower crowns, and the pervading presence of the C-scroll motif, not least in the gallery parapet.

EINSIEDELN (SW)   Klosterkirche

104, 105   In 1749 an anonymous builder provided two identical-looking Epistle and Gospel organs to flank the choir entrance of this monastery church. Once again it is certainly not the rigid lines of the cases (apart from the concave end compartments) but the applied decoration which gives them their Rococo flavour (though alterations may have taken place in 1773–6). The over-large putti were carved by Johann Baptist Babel, who may in fact have been responsible for the design of the cases as a whole.

SANKT FLORIAN (A)   Stiftskirche

106   An unusual-looking case designed 1770–4 by Johann Christian Jegg to house an instrument built by Franz Xaver Chrismann. One cannot feel entirely happy about Jegg's creation. The vertical and horizontal lines of the case are surely too strong for the Rococo pipe shades and other extraneous decoration, which are consequently swamped. Nor was it a good idea to bring the two main towers up to a somewhat hesitant peak. Originally the central flat and its two supporting sections were much lower (i.e. up to the height of the supporting herms) and was not raised to its present height until 1875. On the whole the present height would seem to be preferable.

    Anton Bruckner was organist here from 1848 until 1855 and lies buried in a crypt beneath the organ at which he spent so many happy hours.

SCHWYZ (SW)   Sankt Martin

107   Built 1778–80 by Franz Joseph Bouthillier of Dinkelsbühl, the case designed (or perhaps only constructed) by Felix Schilliger. At first sight this organ has visually more in common with much older instruments in both Germany and the Netherlands, notably in the arrangement of its towers and flats and the division of the latter into tiers. Only the pleasantly fluid lines of its front plan and some elements of the decoration (e.g. the use of the C-scroll motif—though this is more immediately apparent in the gallery parapet than in the pipe shades) mark it out as being of the later eighteenth century.

NERESHEIM (G)   Klosterkirche

108   This architectural case designed round a six-light west window inevitably recalls Weingarten (83–5). But the builder, Johann Nepomuk Holzhay, was no Gabler, and moreover by 1797, the date of the organ, the style of decoration had changed radically from the extravagance of the Baroque to the restraint of Neo-classicism. Given these facts, it must be admitted that on the whole Holzhay has done a good job here. Indeed it could be said that he has succeeded in merging the organ so successfully with its architectural surroundings that it has lost its visual identity altogether.

HOF-AN-DER-SAALE (G)   Sankt Michaelis

109   A mock-medieval case housing an organ of 1834 built by the brothers Heidenreich. Its flimsy façade and unthinking mixture of medieval architectural and decorative elements point unerringly to its period.

GIENGEN-AN-DER-BRENZ (G)   Sankt Marien

110   A not unpleasant pseudo-Rococo/Classical pastiche built 1905 by the brothers Link of Giengen. Unfortunately the wobbly line of the pipe mouths is an unsettling element that spoils the total effect.

Denmark

SORØ Klosterkirke

This case probably started life in the sixteenth century looking much as it does now. It is,   111
however, a reconstruction based on careful research and attention to such clues as it already
contained. In 1627–8 it was moved from elsewhere in the church to its present position at the
west end by Johann Lorenz, who apparently retained the main Gothic structure though
adding a *Positiv*. In 1774 it was drastically updated in Rococo style. Restoration in 1942
revealed amongst other things that there had once been shutters, that some of the display
pipes had originally been mounted in mirror formation, and that only the central tower
remained from the original Gothic case. New pipe shades were modelled on those of the
Positiv; this, having been emptied of its functional pipes during a rebuild of 1846, was found to
contain the impressive heraldic device and four decorative crests which now adorn the main
case.

ROSKILDE Domkirke

The main case may be said to date from 1654 (the date given over the right-hand front flat).   112
The general design, style and detail are typically Baroque (in particular the very wide side-
pieces and the elaborate tower crowns). On the other hand the case is in fact an enlargement
of an earlier one built in 1555 by the Netherlands master Hermann Rafaelis Rodensteen Pock,
and indeed the *Positiv* is as he built it except for the addition of elaborate Baroque figures and
ornament on top. The similarity of its angular plan to those of the *Positiv* cases at, e.g.
Enkhuizen and 's-Hertogenbosch (8, 12) may clearly be seen. The three-dimensional medallion heads on the gallery front are of the same period (cf. 44), though the elaborate *cul-de-
lampe* is again an obvious Baroque addition.

HILLERØD Frederiksborg Slotskirke

A world-famous chamber organ, designed entirely for secular use and completed about 1610   113
by Esias Compenius in consultation with the composer Michael Praetorius, who describes the
instrument in volume II (1619) of his lengthy treatise on contemporary music and musical
instruments, *Syntagma Musicum*. It was originally built as a commission from the Duke of
Braunschweig-Wolfenbüttel in North Germany, with whom Praetorius was then in service,
and was not presented to King Christian IV of Denmark until 1616. Compenius accompanied
it to Frederiksborg but died there soon after supervising its installation in 1617.

   This seems to have been a rare if not unique instance of the case (here made of oak, finely
carved and richly decorated in the best High Renaissance manner) having preceded the
actual instrument, which Compenius had then to fit into the space at his disposal. That he
managed to do this, and at the same time to produce an organ having two manuals and pedals
and some twenty-seven speaking stops, is a tribute to his genius and skill.

   The organ contains 1001 pipes, all of wood, and of these only two (set in the display front) are dummies. The display pipes themselves are faced with ivory and have ebony ornamentation round the mouths. The use of ebony and ivory for the black and white keys on the manuals is also extended to the pedalboard, which can be pushed into the body of the instrument when not in use. The drawstop knobs are of solid silver and are mainly in the form of human and animal heads.

Thanks to years of neglect the instrument is almost unaltered and has been restored to full playing order. No other extant organ of the period approaches so nearly the sound of the Renaissance dance band which the organ builders tried to imitate. Among its special effects are two tremulants, bagpipes and 'a little humming bee stop' (Praetorius).

HILLERØD Frederiksborg Slotskirke

114 A nineteenth-century reconstruction of the original early seventeenth-century organ, begun by Nikolaus Maas and completed by Johann Lorenz, only to be totally destroyed by fire in 1859 together with most of the other contents of the Castle (though not, happily, the Compenius organ which at that time was not in the chapel).

The reconstruction shows us that it was a late Renaissance case of great ornamental vigour, especially in the huge *culs-de-lampe* and the numerous carved figures; however, those on top of the towers are too small to compete for attention with the indigestible ceiling ornament. The ear-like side-pieces containing display pipes are an unusual and slightly disturbing feature.

HADERSLEV Domkirke

115 Built in 1652 by Peter Karstensen Botz, who has evidently taken his design—with its pedal towers coming forward into the gallery parapet—from the 'Hamburg front' school. A highly unusual feature, however, is the use of actual pipes to form the front vertical edges of the pedal towers. The quietly harmonious proportions of this case as a whole (carefully restored in 1947) are especially notable.

KØBENHAVN Vor Frelsers Kirke

116 A case carved from unpainted oak and maple by Christian Nerger of Saxony to house an instrument built 1698–1700 by the brothers Johann and Peter Petersen Botzen. The totally Baroque character of this case is revealed not only in the richness and style of its decoration but in the frequent servile references to King Christian v—the bust housed in the *Positiv*, the crowned monogram on top of the central tower, and the inscription carried by the central pipe in each of the five towers, 'Deo et C.5 Gloria'. In the actual design of the case a faint echo of the 'Hamburg' type might be traced in the way the end towers descend below the impost, though they are not united to the gallery. The tin display pipes are ornamented in cast pewter. The carvings of musical instruments on the *Positiv* are especially good.

This organ is the only important one of its period in the city to have escaped the fires which swept København in 1728 and in 1798. The elephants which can be glimpsed beneath the *Positiv*, sculptured in relief on either side of the entrance doors, perhaps refer punningly both to the heavy case which they seemingly support and also to the Order of the Elephant, Denmark's highest award then but newly instituted.

KØBENHAVN Holmens Kirke

117 Built 1740 by Lambert Daniel Kastens. His apprenticeship to Arp Schnitger is visually reflected in the organ's obvious indebtedness to the 'Hamburg' design, with modifications (cf. 24, the organ at Zwolle by Johann Georg and Franz Caspar Schnitger). Four of Kastens's cases remain in Denmark, three in København and the fourth in the Domkirke at Aarhus, and

all show the same characteristics, although details such as the extent of carving on the side-pieces may differ. Here in the Holmens Kirke the overall design is notably compact and well proportioned.

ODENSE Domkirke
Built in 1752 by Amdi Worm, of København and Jutland. This seems to have been his largest   118
instrument. The case could be said to be derived from the 'Hamburg' type (obviously highly influential in Denmark), but the wide central tower resting on a simple bracket and connected to the pedal towers by concave flats is unusual, and neatly offsets the incurving of the gallery and central section of the *Positiv*. Although the decoration is at first sight of the later Baroque era, the emergent Rococo style is present in the C-scroll composition of the side-pieces and *culs-de-lampe* beneath the *Positiv*, and also in the naturalistic vases on top of the latter's towers.

France

STRASBOURG   Cathédrale Notre-Dame

119   Case made in 1489–91 by Friedrich Krebs of Ansbach to house his own instrument, later replaced. He built it on the site of an earlier organ, high up on the wall of the north nave and at a considerable distance from the choir. The general design and much of the carving remains from this period. However, in 1712 Andreas Silbermann was asked to rebuild the organ, and although his demand for an entirely new case was successfully resisted he did provide new pipe shades for the flanking compartments of the main case, the elaborate side-pieces and the volute supports below the impost, and new display pipes whose mouths at different levels destroyed the single plane which is such a feature of original Gothic ones. In introducing the side-pieces Silbermann also removed the shutters of both the main case and the *Positif*, and these are now lost.

PERPIGNAN   Cathédrale Saint-Jean

120   It is hard to believe that this case dates from *c.* 1500, as it is reputed to do, even allowing for alterations to pipe shades and display pipes that apparently took place during the nineteenth century. On the other hand, it is obviously Spanish-influenced in design (cf. 167) and at the time it was built Perpignan was a Spanish possession. It is situated on the north side of the nave near the choir.

AMIENS   Cathédrale Notre-Dame

121   A Renaissance case of 1549–52, though in its design possibly dating back to an earlier Gothic instrument of 1422. The *Positif* case, however, is later, 1620–2. The pavilion-like structures on top of the towers originally housed figures of King David and attendant angels, and there were also wings of an apparently later date, but all these items vanished at some time during the nineteenth-century, or possibly when the organ was dismantled at the beginning of the First World War. The horizontal arrangement of the pipe mouths has long since been lost, and the outlines of the case are spoiled by the modern swell box situated behind the central tower.

TOURS   Cathédrale Saint-Gatien

122   A fine Renaissance case, said to be of 1562, whose three main towers have probably been lengthened; the additional lengths can be judged from the extra pieces added on above the fluted pilasters which form such an important part of the whole architectural design. The hooded caps of the two end towers are a curious feature. The trumpeting angels on the pavilions over the two smaller towers were originally moveable, while the figures on the central tower are, unusually, those of the Roman legionary saints Maurice, Candidus and Exuperius.

   The *Positif* case, as its style and decoration indicate, is of later date, either 1611 or 1617. Somewhat unusual are the two-tiered convex flats at the sides (but cf. 129).

LA FERTÉ-BERNARD   Notre-Dame-des-Marais

Case built in 1536 (date above the central flat) by the cabinet-maker Sainctot Chemin to   123
house an instrument by Pierre Bert of Le Mans. Ingenious compression has meant that a
front which would normally be strung out lengthwise has been angled and drawn together so
as to fit inside one of the arches in the north wall of the nave. The elaborate and angular
gallery originally supported an earlier organ of *c.* 1500. It hangs high up on the wall in the
manner of a 'swallow's nest'.

SAINT-BERTRAND-DE-COMMINGES   Cathédrale Notre-Dame

A rare if not unique example of a case being built within a right-angle. The date is 1536, the   124
carver Nicolas Bachelier. Classical pilasters and half-columns are again used as the vertical
divisions of the case. Another unusual feature is the fact that the two end towers do not rise
above the cornice but are contained by it. All five towers (including the two very small
V-shaped ones) are crowned by the lanterns that seem to be a normal feature of French
Renaissance cases, although alterations to them may have taken place *c.* 1900. The organist
reaches his bench beneath the central tower by way of a winding staircase that is incorporated
into the whole structure and can be seen at the right-hand side.

CAUDEBEC-EN-CAUX   Notre Dame

Main case built 1542–3 to house an instrument by Antoine-Josseline and Gilbert Cocquerel of   125
Rouen. It harmonises unusually well with the architecture of the church which was not
completed until 1539, and has obviously been designed in accordance with Renaissance
theories of 'harmonic proportions'. The divisions between the compartments are here formed
by female musicians. The crowning lanterns are superb, and we may note also the shrine-like
structures over the three flats.

   The *Positif* was added in 1740, and considering its distance in time from the main case is
surprisingly successful, both in its proportions and in the fact that it does not distract attention
away from the main case.

CHARTRES   Cathédrale Notre-Dame

The origins of this magnificent case are said to lie in a Gothic organ of 1475 which was con-   126
structed in this awe-inspiring and vertiginous position high up on the south wall of the nave.
From this earliest organ may come the gallery and possibly also the side towers (originally
single-tier). However, the case probably took on its basic aspect in 1542–51, when the
instrument was enlarged by Robert Fillcul and the case altered to fit it by the cabinet-
makers Rolland Foubert and Jacques Bely. Subsequent alterations were carried out at different
times during the succeeding centuries, but precise details of these are either confused or
lacking. The important thing surely is that the case is as much an architectural *tour-de-force*
as is the great cathedral that shelters it.

LES ANDELYS   Notre-Dame du Grand Andely

Built 1573 by Nicolas Dabenet, in a similar style to that at Caudebec (125). Here however   127
the carving is superior, notably the relief panels of muscial instruments above the flats, and
those of Old Testament figures below the impost, and the relief groups on the gallery parapet,
amongst which are four from that typically Renaissance group, the Seven Liberal Arts. Only
two details mar the composition as a whole—the continuation of the cornice line just above
the flats round the pipes of the end towers, and the interruption of the sequence of horizontals
by the different levels of the non-original display pipes.

RODEZ   Cathédrale Notre-Dame

128   The 1628 case was built for an instrument by Antoine Vernholles of Poitiers and carved (at least in part) by Raymond Gusmond of Périgueux. The heavy and in some places even crude carving is a disappointment, in idiom late Renaissance verging on Baroque. The actual design of the case looks back to the Renaissance proper in the inevitable tower lanterns and elaborate *culs-de-lampe* beneath the towers of both the main and *Positif* cases.

The most noticeable feature of this design is its insistence on towers at the expense of the flats which consequently become so narrow that some contain no more than four pipes, some only three. There are seven towers, and it has been suggested that these are deliberately symbolic of the Seven Joys and Sorrows of the Blessed Virgin Mary to whom the cathedral is dedicated.

TOULOUSE   Cathédrale Saint-Étienne

129   Case designed *c.* 1611 by Pierre Monge of Narbonne to house an instrument by Antoine Lefebvre; carving by Louis Bihorri and Antoine Moréjot. The flowing movement of this front anticipates the Baroque, although the pilasters topped by obelisks which terminate it at each side are a Renaissance feature. The end towers (echoed by those of the *Positif*) are rounded and the angular silhouette of the tower caps is avoided by the linking gallery. The arched pipe shades of the *Positif* may be nineteenth-century replacements rather than original, and the visually boring substructure also points to interference from the same period.

EMBRUN   Notre-Dame

130   A not unhandsome but hybrid case consisting of a Gothic (1463) substructure and a mainly eighteenth-century superstructure and (probably) *Positif*. The centre tower is perhaps a trifle too high, and it is unusual to find pipes displayed at the side of a case as well as in the front.

ROUEN   Saint-Ouen

131   Case dated 1630, built for an instrument by Crespin Carlier. Unique in France if not in Europe as a whole, its unusual appearance is due to the arched toe-boards and to the upward and outward incline of the curving pipe shades; this gives a strong sensation of thrusting outward toward the end towers. In fact the pipe shades of the flats have, as it were, been turned upside down with the carving above. The figures on the towers, apart from those of angels, are of Christ with King David and St Cecilia (playing a small positive). Domes, round or faceted, now become a familiar feature of many French organ towers.

LA FLÈCHE   Chapelle Saint-Louis du Prytanée Militaire

132   Case built 1638–40 by Pierre Frilleux and Pierre Cornet, cabinet-makers of Angers, for an instrument by Ambroise Levasseur. It has been suggested that this case contains elements of an earlier one of 1622 which is known to have been in the chapel, though not on this gallery which was not built until *c.* 1635. Certainly the tops of the end compartments (which in a typical French design of this period should normally be rounded) impinge cruelly upon the lantern turrets of the towers. The carved decoration is for the most part vigorously Baroque; especially notable are the side supports of the main superstructure, the central *cul-de-lampe* of the same, and the supporting volutes of the central tower. The angels on the half-pediments have lost their trumpets, and further casualties are the shutters of both main and *Positif* cases. But a unusual compensatory bonus is the retention of the original gilding and colours of blue and pale pink.

PARIS   Saint-Étienne-du-Mont

Instrument completed 1636 by Pierre Pescheur, case by the cabinet-maker Jean Buron. The   133
design is especially notable for the unusual composition of the flats including the partial
division into two tiers. There is much fine carving, including the figures of Christ and angels
on the main case, and supporting figures at the sides, cherubs on the *Positif*, and relief panels
of Biblical subjects on the main case and gallery parapet.

REIMS   Cathédrale Notre-Dame

The present case was reconstructed in 1620–47 from a late Gothic case of which there are   134
now no visible reminders except the gallery (1468). Some of the impact of the main case has
been lost by the later removal of the small pipes in the wreathed compartments in the upper
tier of flats; the effect of these can to some extent be judged by looking at the *Positif* where the
same idea has been followed, though in other respects the *Positif* does not much resemble the
main case. The carved decoration is early Baroque in spirit.

PARIS   Saint-Merry

Case completed *c.* 1651 by the cabinet-maker Germain Pillon. The towers of the main case,   135
topped by scaled domes (another typically French feature), are so arranged as to admit light
from the west window, and wreathed compartments of tiny dummy pipes are again introduced as at Reims (134). In the *Positif*, conventional pipe shades are replaced by carved
drapes with tasselled lappets; these may date from 1719 when the display pipes were altered.
The clock is a still later addition, and the gallery itself dates from *c.* 1750. The original winged
figures supporting the end towers are especially fine.

LES ANDELYS   Saint-Sauveur du Petit-Andely

Originally built 1674 for a convent, by Robert Ingout of Cherbourg, and installed at   136
Saint-Sauveur in 1793 at the west end. The silhouette is spoiled by the upper gallery (the
lower having come with the organ from the convent). To the French convention of scaled
domes is added another, that of topping them with vases and plumes.

LA CHAISE-DIEU   Saint-Robert

A late seventeenth-century case heavily and characteristically carved in the Baroque manner.   137
The end towers of the main case are topped by figures of angels which cannot be seen in the
illustration; similar figures, however, may be glimpsed above the *Positif* supporting the same
towers.

   The *Positif* itself bears the date 1683, but its appearance is so unlike that of the main case
that it seems doubtful the two can have been designed together. The *Positif* design fails
completely to show the homogeneity which distinguishes the main case; it is far too wide and
unnecessarily fragmented into tiered flats of minute display pipes (not original).

AUCH   Cathédrale Sainte-Marie

A well-balanced Baroque case designed to contain an instrument built 1690–4 by Jean de   138
Joyeuse. The galleried turrets on the principal towers look back, however, to an earlier style.
Our old friends David and St Cecilia are present again; together with Saul they appear
carved in relief on the substructure. The central figure on the main case is that of the Virgin,
on the *Positif* St Augustine.

MARMOUTIER   Église Abbatiale

A classic example both visually and tonally of the work of Andreas Silbermann, built 1709–10.   139

The general design is simplicity itself, the decoration restrained though rich; especially notable though less immediately obvious are the relief friezes of acanthus carved on the impost of the main case and at the base of the *Positif*. In contrast the side-pieces (of which Silbermann made a feature—cf. 119) proclaim themselves immediately and confidently. Unfortunately the design suffers from the effect of the wooden pedal pipes rising up above the main case.

VERSAILLES Château, Chapelle Saint-Louis

140 The extreme richness of this case is explained by its situation. Only the most sumptuous-looking organ would suffice to adorn the palace chapel of the Sun King, Louis XIV. The case was originally designed *c.* 1700 by the royal architect Jules-Hardouin Mansart, together with the rest of the chapel furnishings and fittings, though this design was partly altered by Mansart's successor Robert de Cotte. Into it was built, 1709–10, an instrument by Robert Cliquot.

Like all other pieces of royal French furniture this organ case was a synthesis of the work of several different craftsmen including the cabinet-maker Marteau, the sculptor Bertrand and the carver Dugoulon. In itself it is unique, and moreover occupies a most unusual site immediately over the altar facing the royal box (a more suitable word, in the context of this theatrical setting, than 'pew').

SAINT-OMER Notre-Dame

141 Cases and gallery were provided in 1717 by Jean and Antoine-Joseph Piette of Saint-Omer, a carver and cabinet-maker respectively, for an organ by two more brothers, Thomas and Jean-Jacques Desfontaines of Douai. This is a fine case which sweeps forward and upward in confident curves but which is somewhat overwhelmed by the carved figures which stand on and around it. These include David and St Cecilia (end towers of the main case) and Faith and Hope (detached figures beneath the same towers). The *Positif* repeats the central section of the main case.

AIX-EN-PROVENCE Cathédrale Saint-Sauveur

142 A dummy front which faces the almost identical façade of the organ across the choir, in imitation of Italian practice (of some influence in this region). The organ itself was built in 1744–6 by Jean-Esprit Isnard of Tarascon. Notable features of this case are the flaming urns on top of the towers and the delicate relief panels of musical instrument trophies on the sub-structure. The actual arrangement of flats and pipes, however, seems rather dull, though the inspiration behind the decoration is Rococo. The original display pipes of this dummy case have, unusually, been preserved (though not those of the organ proper). The delicate tracery of the wrought-iron gallery parapet should not be ignored.

UZÈS Saint-Théodorit

143 If still all original, as it seems to be, this is a remarkably well-preserved anonymous case of *c.* 1685, complete with shutters (canvas on wooden frames), in themselves a late survival for this period. The case colours of light grey and gold are also said to be original. If the *Positif* seems over-wide this is because it is obviously intended to be a miniature (though not completely identical) reflection of the main case. This being so, it does look as though the two-handled covered cups on the outer towers of the main case, though also typical of the period, might be replacements for the equally typical vases of fruit and flowers which appear on the other towers of both cases. The display pipes are from a rebuild in 1841–3.

This photograph was taken before restoration of the organ in 1961–4.

BAYONNE   Cathédrale Sainte-Marie

There seems no reason to doubt that this case is basically of the eighteenth century; on the   144
other hand the organ was rebuilt in 1865 and the case may then also have been rearranged and
added to. Certainly what could have been quite a graceful outline has been completely
ruined by the addition of swell boxes behind the main tower. The carved details, also, are too
diverse to be completely convincing.

ÉBERSMUNSTER   Église Abbatiale

By Andreas Silbermann, completed 1732, his largest instrument after that of Strasbourg (119),   145
and one of the only two of his many (about 35) organs to survive intact. As is usual with
Silbermann, both the design and the decoration of the case are conservative and restrained.
Compared with his case at Marmoutier (139) this is obviously broader, the front plan being
U–U–U–U–U rather than a simple U–U–U. But the decorative side-pieces are present in both
examples, the acanthus leaf motif is re-used, and the style of the pipe shades is the same. At
Ébersmunster Silbermann also provided the carved upper half of the gallery parapet, portions
of which form sliding panels.

ALBI   Cathédrale Sainte-Cécile

Built in 1736 by Christophe Moucherel of Toul. The unusual width of both main and *Positif*   146
cases does not seem amiss in this context, although the late Baroque decoration perhaps fails
to merge satisfactorily with the painted Gothic and other ornament and tableaux surrounding
it. The figures include those of SS Cecilia and Valerian (the former's far less well-known
husband) on the towers flanking the main central one; the musical putti on the *Positif* are
charming and their instruments include the less usual serpent and bagpipes.

DIJON   Cathédrale Saint-Bénigne

Case constructed 1743 by Edmé Marlet, cabinet-maker, to house an instrument by Karl   147
Joseph Riepp. There is no hint here of the visual wonders of Ottobeuren (92–5), though they
are faintly suggested in the upward-curving pipe shades of the outer flats (main case) and the
relief trophies of musical instruments. Nevertheless there is a sense of flow and movement
about this case, expressed most strongly in the forward concavity of the outer flats and the
anti-movement of the *Positif*'s upper outline as well as in its trefoliated central tower.

VERSAILLES   Château, Cabinet du Dauphin

Chamber organ attributed to Nicolas Somer and said to have been the property of Queen   148
Marie-Antoinette. After the Revolution it was placed in the church of Saint-Sulpice, Paris
(from which period this photograph dates) and did not return to Versailles until 1969.

   The organ dates from *c.* 1745 and the casework may be by Jacques Verberckt, who was
employed at the palace during that period. Its Rococo style and its regal affiliations are plain
to see and require no further comment, except that the cluster of pipes at each end of the case
is unusual in a church organ and even more so in a chamber instrument (but cf. 115).

   The keyboards are modern and the rest of the instrument dates back no further than the
1860s.

NANCY   Cathédrale Notre-Dame

Built 1756–7 to a design by the royal architect Jean Nicolas Jennesson, for an organ by Joseph   149
and Nicolas Dupont. A restless, segmental façade in the Rococo manner, with some areas
concave, including the central compartment. As so often happens the silhouette has been
spoiled at a later date by the clutter of pipes and swell box behind it.

PARIS   Saint-Gervais-et-Saint-Protais

150   Dating in its present form from 1758–9, the case contains elements of an earlier one, 1601. The eighteenth-century appearance was given it by Pierre-Claude Thiessé, cabinet-maker, and Fichon and Leblanc, carvers. Likewise the *Positif*, though dating basically from 1659, was enlarged in 1764 by Nicolas Rébillé. Its flats contain display pipes dating from the 1601 instrument, but those of the main case are *c.* 1760. The appearance of the main case is not helped by the wooden pipes (also 1760), which can be seen at the sides, outside the case itself.

François Couperin Le Grand was organist here 1687–1723 (he had the case shutters removed), as were also Armand-Louis and Gervais-François Couperin. The instrument narrowly escaped destruction both in the Revolution and the First World War.

SAINT-MAXIMIN-LA-SAINTE-BAUME   Sainte-Marie-Madeleine

151   The organ case, the instrument itself, the gallery and its supports and staircase were the work of Jean-Esprit Isnard of Tarascon, aided by his nephew Jean-Baptiste and a band of craftsmen. It seems incredible that all this could have been achieved in a single year, but the contract was signed in 1772 and the work completed in 1773.

The main case curves slightly forward, as so many of this period seem to do (cf. 141, 147, 149, 153); this is complemented by the slight backward curve of the *Positif*. Highly original are the curiously-shaped tower caps which also help to give an illusionistic impression of movement. The Rococo style and feeling of the decoration is modified and directed towards Neo-classicism by the urns on the towers of both cases (that on the central tower of the *Positif* looking uncomfortably like a soup tureen). The *Positif* is a notable anti-reflection of the main case, not only in the arrangement of flats and towers but also in the lines of the pipe mouths.

BORDEAUX   Saint-Seurin

152   Case completed 1773 by Messrs Boyé, Burguet, Cabirol and Cessy—cabinet-maker, carpenter and carvers respectively. The instrument was by Jean-Baptiste Micot of Toulouse. Probably the most immediately arresting feature of the case is its forward-thrusting plan which, combined with the falling away of the slightly concave flats, gives the impression of a ship's prow. In fact the design probably owes more to the actual situation of the case, jammed in as it is beneath the west end arches of the church, than to anything else. The carving, however, is of noticeably high quality throughout.

PARIS   Saint-Sulpice

153   Case completed 1779 to a design by Jean-François Chalgrin, better known as the architect of the Arc de Triomphe, for an instrument by François-Henri Cliquot. For the most part classical in its decoration, it is also a classic example of how not to design an organ case, and was recognised as such as soon as it was built. An organ cannot be expected to speak properly when, among other things, its pipe mouths are obstructed by figures and its front is recessed instead of being flat or convex. However, Chalgrin totally disregarded the needs of the instrument and forced it into a preconceived architectural strait-jacket in which the conventional flats and towers are replaced by a temple-like structure formed from classical columns complete with their entablature. The introduction of pipes into each end of the substructure—partially obscured as they are by *culs-de-lampe*—is aesthetically indefensible. The main figures including the central one of King David (here more reminiscent of a Druidic bard than the old-style representation) are said to be by Duret, who also carved the case.

In 1857 Aristide Cavaillé-Coll carried out a rebuild which included a reduction in the number of display pipes, the addition of a swell box which ruined the silhouette of the crowning group, the cutting away of the pipe tops in the *Positif* (to afford the organist at

Cavaillé-Coll's new console a view of the High Altar) and the placing over them of a clock supported by putti. However desirable these changes may have been thought at the time, they cannot be said to have improved the general appearance of the organ.

C. M. Widor and Marcel Dupré were both organists here.

SAINT-GUILHEM-LE-DÉSERT   Église Abbatiale

By Jean-Pierre Cavaillé (grandfather of Aristide Cavaillé-Coll), and left uncompleted at the Revolution, 1789. A competent if unremarkable case; though its proportions are quite well balanced (and would be even better if the substructure were not quite so high), the extremely narrow arch into which it is wedged at the west end succeeds in making it look uncomfortably squashed. At the time this photograph was taken, decorative urns on the end towers had been temporarily removed.

In its general appearance and the pyramidal arrangement of its flats and towers this case is strongly reminscent of English examples of the period 1660–1800.

154

PITHIVIERS   Saint-Salomon-et-Saint-Grégoire

Built 1784–9 by Jean-Baptiste Isnard of Orléans, who had assisted his uncle Jean-Esprit Isnard during the building of the organ at Saint-Maximin-la-Sainte-Baume (151). A fine composition, given a sense of movement unusual for its date by means of the flowing, almost liquid line of the impost in conjunction with the contrapuntal lines of pipe mouths and shades.

155

ORLÉANS   Cathédrale Sainte-Croix

Reputedly from an abbey church at Saint-Benôit-sur-Loire, where it was erected in 1703–6, being moved to Orléans in 1822.

It is difficult to say how much of the present case was part of the original and how much dates from 1822. It would seem reasonable to suppose that the figures (including the supporting Atlases) are from 1703, but that the curious tasselled tower decorations and scrolled pipe shades are nineteenth century. Once again the main outline is spoiled by swell box and free-standing pipes.

156

POITIERS   Cathédrale Saint-Pierre

Case completed 1789 by Pierre Favre, cabinet-maker, and a carver named Berthon, for an instrument by François-Henri Cliquot who died before its completion (it remains an almost unique example of his best work). The case, unremarkable in design, is justly famed for the high quality of its carving which brings to mind the work of Grinling Gibbons and his school in England, though it is of course of much later date.

157

PARIS   Sainte-Marie-Madeleine ('La Madeleine')

Designed by the architect of the church, Jean-Jacques-Marie Huvé, and dating from 1844–6; carving by Antoine-André Marneuf. The best thing that can be said for this case is that it allows the pipes to speak. The organ itself was an early work by Aristide Cavaillé-Coll, and organists at the church have included Saint-Saëns and Fauré.

The main influence behind this case seems to have been a mixture of the Italian and Spanish traditions.

158

PARIS   Saint-Eustache

Designed 1849 by Victor Baltard for an instrument by Messrs Ducroquet. The plan of the main case is interesting, but that of the *Positif* could hardly be less so, and the entire composition seems to be weighed down by the enormous mass of figures and architectural features

159

on top. The main figures, by Eugène Guillaume, represent St Cecilia in the centre, with Saul (left) about to hurl a javelin at David on the opposite tower.

PARIS Sainte-Clotilde

160 Designed *c.* 1857 by the architect of the church, F. C. Gau, the organ itself by Aristide Cavaillé-Coll, completed 1859. An ugly, angular case, whose decoration and idiom is no more like the original Gothic it strives to suggest than Huvé's case at La Madeleine (158) resembles a genuine Italian or Spanish Renaissance case. César Franck was organist here from 1858 until his death in 1890.

Spain, Portugal

SALAMANCA (S)   Catedral Vieja, Capilla de San Bartolomé

It is somewhat misleading to call this the oldest organ in Spain, as is sometimes claimed, since   161
there remains nothing of it except the case and bellows. There can be no doubt that the small
castellated case is ancient, possibly as old as the gallery which dates from *c*. 1370. The painting
on it, however, is later and of the Renaissance, *c*. 1480. Perhaps the most interesting feature
to survive are the bellows, which are double and protrude behind the case; this is the manner
in which the larger positives were blown, and this organ may be regarded as a transitional
instrument between the positive and the immobile church organ proper.

ZARAGOSA (S)   Catedral de la Seo

These plates present the two faces of the double-sided case situated above the stalls in the   162, 163
choir, plate 162 showing the aisle frontage. The date is usually put at 1443, and the crafts-
manship is attributed to Moorish artists. However, there is not much Moorish influence to be
seen in the case, except possibly in the tent-like pinnacles on top of the towers and some of the
lattice-like carved panels below the main compartments (though these panels may be of later
date) of the choir case. The latter is unusually large for the period; it is the aisle front which
most has the appearance of a true Gothic case. It has painted wooded accretions including at
each side panels of 'pipes' with grotesque faces painted round their mouths; all this seems
also to be of later date.

   In assessing Iberian organ cases it should always be remembered that the horizontal reed
pipes protruding at impost level from so many instruments (*en chamade*), their overpowering
tone so characteristic of a country of strong and colourful contrasts, cannot possibly be
earlier than the mid-seventeenth century, and most old extant examples are of the eighteenth.

CALATAYUD (S)   San Pedro de los Francos

A fine late Gothic 'swallow's nest' gallery supporting a case of *c*. 1480, typically Gothic in its   164
flat frontage, its tripartite arrangement of flats, and the style of its openwork pipe shades and
impost frieze. It has, however, lost its shutters, and some form of decoration is missing from the
blank areas above each of the compartments. The display pipes appear to be original and have
retained the traditional linear arrangement of their mouths.

TOLEDO (S)   Catedral

Perhaps the most unusual feature of this case is the material from which it is made—stone.   165
However, even its general appearance is very probably unique. The design was by the
architect Alonso de Covarrubias, who also provided a number of buildings in Toledo, and the
case was completed in 1539. It has been conceived less as an organ case than as an architectural
continuation of the screen below, which frames the so-called 'Lion Porch' and stands in the
south transept. Even the case itself is in the nature of a graceful arcaded screen—it is certainly
not an organ case in the accepted sense of the word.

SALAMANCA (s)   Catedral Nueva

166   This is the aisle side of the double-fronted 'old' organ of the cathedral, situated on the Epistle side of the choir (on the right as one faces the altar), and was almost certainly brought here from the still extant former cathedral in 1568 or 1569. It is said to date from 1558. It has obvious similarities in appearance to Renaissance cases elsewhere in Europe; details include the three-tower design, the stepped pipe shades and the decoration. The triangular pediments with three-dimensional carved heads are especially reminiscent of Enkhuizen (8, 9), though being of course much larger. (Note also the heads in roundels on the arch above.) The wings were painted by Francisco de Montejo of Toledo with figures of SS James and John on the exterior, SS Peter and Paul on the interior. Carving was by Antonio Tarza.

BARCELONA (s)   Catedral

167   Case dated 1539–41 and made by Antonio Carbonelli. A cliff-like erection of Renaissance carving with 'windows' let in for display pipes. The latter, which are not all original, have been rearranged in modern times in a manner which allows far too much space between them. The *Positivo* does not seem to belong to the grand design at all.

EVORA (P)   Catedral

168   The oldest organ in Portugal, 1562, situated in the nave near the choir. A glance is enough to show that the case is strongly influenced by Italian Renaissance sources, either at first-hand or via the medium of engraved plates. The architectural design and the pyramidal arrangement of the pipes without shades are typically Italian—in fact the only visual feature which is not is the *Trompeta Real*, its pipes arranged *en chamade* as usual, and this was an eighteenth-century addition.

TARRAGONA (s)   Catedral

169–71   Another great cliff-like case designed in the early 1560s by Jayme Amigó. The overall design is architectural in character, based firmly on the principles of the Italian Renaissance, the carved decoration itself late Renaissance (170). While the display front may perhaps remind one of the façade of an Italian Renaissance church, the entire composition including the huge wings (painted 1563 by Pedro Sefarí and Pedro Pablo of Montalbergo with scenes from the Life of Christ) is more reminiscent of one of those large altarpieces for which the Iberian peninsula is noted. Indeed one cannot and should not ignore the influence of these highly venerated items of church furniture on the design of Iberian organ cases in general.

   The *Positivo* (171) exemplifies in miniature the typically Renaissance architectural approach as well as the established use of three-dimensional heads (see also those on the surrounding gallery). The sinuous carved dolphins on top of the curved pediment are a typical expression of Renaissance secularity.

HUESCA (s)   Catedral

172   This box-like case situated in the nave (Epistle side), though apparently containing elements of a much earlier one (1585), was put together in its present form in 1761. Its Rococo ornamentation by Antonio Sanz of Zaragosa is too fragmented to make much impact on the viewer except one of irritation, and the disparity between the imitation display pipes in the upper flats and the real ones in the lower is so marked as to be laughable. However, in the general design there has been some attempt to reduce the type of flat front broken up into a number of differently-sized compartments at varying levels, which is such a feature of much Spanish organ case design in general.

ZARAGOSA (S)   Nuestra Señora del Pilar
This case dates from 1527 but its outline was drastically altered in 1950 when it was moved   173
to the west end of the church; originally the three main compartments were of equal height
but were topped by pinnacles of which the central one was highest. With the removal of these
and with other alterations much of its character has been lost, although the wealth of late
Renaissance ornament remains. The original designer was Giovanni di Moreto, a Florentine
carver who as might be expected has obviously left his mark on the Italianate style of decoration, though the actual carving was apparently done by his assistant Esteban Ropie.

SALAMANCA (S)   Museo de la Catedral
A positive organ of c. 1550, perhaps by Damián Luys. Its chief visual attractions are the four   174
relief panels which form the sides; set in architectural framework and standing over panels of
Flemish-style strapwork, they illustrate the Tree of Jesse (over the keyboard), the Assumption, and two heraldic motifs. The absence of visible pipes in this type of organ is less unusual
in Spain than elsewhere.
    The organ still retains its original keyboard and some of the pipework.

CIUDAD RODRIGO (S)   Catedral
The Gospel organ, dating from some time during the seventeenth century. A neatly-   175
balanced little work distinguished by a wealth of fine Baroque carving and by painted panels
round the console. This is designed as a free-standing instrument, having lattice-work grilles
at the sides and back to let the sound out. (For the Epistle organ see 181.)

CÁDIZ (S)   Catedral Nueva
The Gospel organ of c. 1680, transferred from the old cathedral in 1797. Baroque in style   176
and feeling, though the heraldic cartouche on the central tower is perhaps too large, and the
overall design is spoiled by the early eighteenth-century additions of pipes en chamade.

BURGOS (S)   Catedral, Capilla del Condestable
Case designed c. 1530 by the decorator of the chapel, Felipe Vigarny, for an instrument by   177
Ferdinand Ximenez. A highly unusual and individual design for an organ not much bigger
than a positive, decorated in thoroughgoing Renaissance style.

BURGOS (S)   Catedral
The Epistle organ by Juan de Argüeta, completed in 1645 (this is the choir front; that facing   178
onto the aisle behind is in nineteenth-century neo-Gothic style). It would be hard to conceive
of a more uninspiring visual presentation of an organ. The coup-de-grâce is of course the failure
of the large pipes to reach up as far as the shades. Alterations were carried out in 1706 by
José de Echevarría, who added not only pipes en chamade but also a row of carved cherubs'
heads immediately above them, perhaps in imitation of the heads carved on the arches. (For
the Gospel organ see 202.)

BURGOS (S)   Catedral, Capilla de San Enrique
A small organ of c. 1675, looking like a positive but in fact fixed. The case is richly carved in   179
the Flemish interpretation of the High Renaissance. The gallery round the top seems to be
an attempt to integrate the case into the surrounding metal screens which enclose the chapel.
All the display pipes are dummies.

EL BURGO DE OSMA (s)   Catedral

180   The Epistle organ, 1641, by Quintin Mayo of Flanders. The builder's origins explain this organ's obvious affinities with North European styles in the arrangement of flats and towers and the general style of ornament. Unusual features of the design are the small lantern-like structures containing tiny display pipes on top of the central tower and also on the two small inner towers. Quaint musical cherubs stand at the feet of the main display pipes in each end tower. The display pipes themselves appear to be original. Alterations (including the addition of pipes *en chamade*) were made in 1771, and it is possible that some of the decoration dates from this time.

CIUDAD RODRIGO (s)   Catedral

181   The Epistle organ, perhaps designed by the architect Manuel de Lara y Churriguera, who was working in the cathedral *c.* 1735. The only other style of design to which this case can be even vaguely compared is the Italian. Points of interest are the oval display compartments, the two displayed wooden pipes with faces painted round the mouths (just inside the outermost posts of the framework), and, next to these and standing just above the impost, figures of putti holding small bells which can be activated by a drawstop.

The case is heavily overloaded with carved decoration of high quality, and can be easily visualised in a South American church or cathedral. (For the Gospel organ see 175.)

ORIHUELA (s)   Catedral

182   Dated 1734; although anonymous, the case shows closer connection with the mainstream of North European design than many other Spanish examples. However, the conception of a superimposed architectural tabernacle as the crowning feature of the case still remains (this is found also in Italy, though to a lesser extent). The *Positivo* forms a more homogeneous part of the composition than is usual in Spain. The late Baroque decoration also recalls North European sources, especially the carved side-pieces.

TUDELA (s)   Catedral

183   A late seventeenth-century anonymous case on the Epistle side, which in its general appearance contains echoes of North European examples, especially in the volute side supports beneath the impost and the elaborate carved side-pieces. However, the carved decoration is more crowded and in general more crude than anything similar to be found outside Spain.

SEGOVIA (s)   Catedral

184   Here again are identical cases for the Epistle and Gospel organs, except that the Gospel organ (left) is double-fronted, while the Epistle organ shows no pipes on its aisle side except for those in the crowning attic compartment. The Epistle organ was built first, 1702, the imitative Gospel case being built in 1772. On the choir side both cases present well-balanced and unified fronts, to which the very slightly convex end flats impart a sense of movement. The upper attic is not perhaps sufficiently well articulated to the rest of the case, and no amount of fine carving can totally remove suggestions of a dog kennel or rabbit hutch from the viewer's mind.

SANTIAGO DE COMPOSTELA (s)   Catedral

185   Identical Gospel and Epistle cases were built in 1705 and 1709 respectively (this is the Gospel case). The designer was the architect Domingo Antonio de Andrade (who also designed the High Altar of the cathedral), the carvers Miguel de Romay and Antonio Alfonsín, and the organ builder Manuel de la Viña of Salamanca.

The vertiginous effect of these cases is increased by the manner in which the topmost areas of carving are forced forward and outward by the curve of the roof arches above them. These carvings appropriately represent St James as the righteous slayer of infidel Moors (Gospel) and St James the Pilgrim receiving a vision of Our Lady of the Pillar (Epistle). The remaining wealth of Baroque carving threatens to smother the otherwise simple arrangement of tiered flats, very slightly rounded 'towers', and attic storey.

TÚY (S)   Catedral

Epistle and Gospel cases built 1712–15 by Antonio del Pino y Velasco of Palencia and carved   186
by Domingo Rodríguez de Pazos, who also worked at Santiago de Compostela. The design seems to go back to North Germany or the Netherlands for its inspiration (except perhaps for the curious turrets on top), but as usual it is virtually smothered by the exuberant if somewhat crude Baroque carving. (Notice here a mannikin figure at the pipe feet of the farthest tower, and compare 180.)

MONDOÑEDO (S)   Catedral

Epistle and Gospel organs in almost identical cases, designed 1714–22 by Bernabé García   187
Seárez for instruments by Manuel de la Viña. Both are double-fronted (this is the Epistle organ, choir front). The design is simple but satisfying, and except for the round-arched upper compartments of the double tier has obvious affinities with the North European tradition. The carving is good and its use judicious in this context.

BRAGA (P)   Catedral

Here also are two identical cases, sited unusually in the second bay of the nave. Constructed   188, 189
1737–8 by Marceliano de Araújo and painted and gilded by Manuel Furtado of Oporto, they housed instruments by Simon Fontanes of Galicia. The quality and somewhat frenzied extent of their decoration can be judged in plate 189, which also shows the meagreness of the *Positivo* as compared with the main case—an unfortunate feature of Iberian organ cases in general, where there is a *Positivo* at all. The Baroque magnificence of the Braga cases, however, cannot be denied.

ALICANTE (S)   San Nicolás de Bari

It is improbable that the date 1755 inscribed on the *Positivo* refers to the original construction   190
of the main case. On stylistic grounds it seems far more likely that the case is of the early seventeenth century and is a survival from an earlier church (the present one dates from 1616–62). For similar flat, architecturally-conceived and Manneristic façades cf. plates 169 (*c.* 1560) and 178 (1645); the design of a tiered centre flanked by two single-tier end compartments containing tall pipes is common to all.

TOLEDO (S)   Catedral

Epistle organ, case carved by Germán López and dated 1758 for an instrument by Pedro   191
Liborna Echevarría of Madrid. In design it suggests an amalgam of those at Segovia and Santiago de Compostela (see 184, 185); it is double-fronted, this being the choir front. The carving, which features the naturalism and C-scrolls of the Rococo style, is lively and attractive, especially the figures of angel and cherub musicians. (For the Gospel organ see 198.)

PALENCIA (S)   Catedral

The case bears the date 1716 and the name of the organ builder Domingo de Aguirre, who   192, 193
may or may not have designed the case (probably not). The sculptor Alonso Manzano is said

to have supplied a design in 1689, but we cannot know whether this is it or is even based on it.

The type of flat front with rectangular upper storey as used at e.g. Orihuela (182) is here allied with shallow U-towers to produce a slightly more unusual façade. The luxuriant Baroque carving is of high quality, as is shown by the detail (192), which also shows the novel treatment afforded to our old friends David and St Cecilia. King David's harp is of concert proportions, while the Saint, seated on a chair, plays a recognisable positive organ.

The large pipes in the towers have faces painted round the mouths, as at Ciudad Rodrigo (181).

TARAZONA (s)   Catedral

194   A curious though highly individual case of 1766 in which the central composition stands out from a background composed of large bass pipes, the whole being set within a frame decorated with stars and putti in relief which fills the arch. The three-tower design with narrow double-tiered flats and carved crowning ornaments of King David with medallions (showing Palestrina and Victoria) suggests French Neo-classical influence. Unusually for Spain, this is a west-end siting.

BRAGA (P)   Nossa Senhora da Lapa

195   A small but interesting mid-eighteenth-century case in Rococo style, notable especially for the flowing lines of the *Positivo* and its supporting gallery reminiscent of the 'swallow's-nest' type. The end sections of the gallery are not actual extensions of the *Positivo* but merely dummy pipes replacing a gallery rail or parapet.

JAÉN (s)   Catedral

196   Case of the Gospel organ, designed 1778 by Manuel Lopez and José García in a totally French Neo-classical manner.

MÁLAGA (s)   Catedral

197   Epistle and Gospel organs in identical cases designed 1778 by the architect José Martín de Aldehuela, for an instrument built by Julían de la Orden of Cuenca. A towering composition of classical architecture and a restatement in these terms of the type of front used at Segovia (184), though the attic storey takes us back at least as far as the Renaissance case at Tarragona (169). As usual the *Positivo* seems wildly out of proportion. Despite the apparently severely classical aspect of the case, elements of the Rococo can be detected creeping into the decoration, for example the carved cartouche at the apex of the pediment, or the larger pipe shades.

TOLEDO (s)   Catedral

198   Gospel organ, 1796; another identical case was made to replace the Epistle organ (191), but owing to the Napoleonic wars this was never set up. The designer of the Gospel case is unknown, though it may have been the architect Ignacio Haam. The casework was provided by Juan Hernández, cabinet-maker of Toledo, and Mariano Salvatierra, carver; José Verdalonga was the organ builder.

This is a mainly simple Neo-classical tabernacle-type case, austere in appearance except for the sudden irruption of the very Baroque angels and urn on the pediment. The general design and the absence of pipe shades point to Italian influence.

CÁDIZ (s)   Catedral Nueva

199   The Epistle organ, 1862, by Pedro Roquer. This case defies comment.

MAFRA (P) Convento
In this large eighteenth-century church there are no less than six organs to be seen, although   200, 201
one of the cases is now empty. The designers and builders are unknown, though the date of
installation was 1806. In each case a light framework of Neo-classical elements surrounds a
pyramid of large speaking display pipes (*Flautado*). The emphasis is on the vertical and the
cases seem to grow with and out of the architecture into which they are so skilfully blended,
as at Ottobeuren (92–4) in another context.

BURGOS (S) Catedral
The Gospel organ of 1806, facing the 1645 Epistle organ (178). Case by Manuel Cortés of   202
Burgos, instrument by Juan Manuel Betozala. A strange mixture of the classical triumphal
arch with pipe shades formed of Renaissance grotesques, crowned by a Rococo medallion
with attendant angels holding floral swags.

CORIA (S) Catedral
The Gospel organ of 1806; this is a slightly cruder version of the Toledo Gospel organ (198),   203
more especially as regards the figures of the angels. The organ builder was Domingo Florenzano of Seville.

CORIA (S) Catedral
The Epistle organ, 1818, by Antonio Nadar da Ponce. Parts of an earlier case may have been   204
used to create this case which, though obviously based in design on the types already seen at
Toledo and Coria itself (198, 203), is much more lighthearted in feeling and even conveys a
cheerful hint of the fairground.

Italy

BOLOGNA   San Petronio

205, 206   The double-fronted Epistle organ (for the Gospel organ see 222, 223) was built between 1470 and 1483 by Lorenzo di Giacomo of Prato. However, despite its antiquity and the fact that several artists of high calibre were employed on the case, the latter took on in 1686 the Baroque character it now bears and is not typical of the fifteenth century. The arrangement of the display pipes in the original case was probably more like that in the present Gospel organ.

PERUGIA   San Pietro

207   A case of c. 1520; designed and painted by Pompeo d'Anselmo, it housed an earlier instrument of the late fifteenth century. This is the simplest form of Italian Renaissance case, without tiers or pipe shades, the pipes in the three compartments arranged in pyramid form and held in place by decorative braces across the front. The inspiration for the form of this case, which is decorated with Renaissance grotesques and roundels containing paintings of SS Peter and Paul, is the Roman triumphal arch. The carved frieze above the cornice may well be a later addition.

SIENA   Santa Maria della Scala

208   A justly celebrated Renaissance case of c. 1515, carved by Carlo d'Andrea Galletti and brightly painted (chiefly in blue and gold) by Ghino d'Antonio. The design of the case as a whole is attributed to the architect Baldassare Peruzzi, and the builder of the instrument was Giovanni di Antonio Piffaro of Siena.

 This case makes its impact all the more strongly from being placed high up on the Epistle side against a totally flat surface; it does not have to contend with other architectural distractions such as pillars and arches. A round-arched central compartment flanked by smaller ones is basically a normal type of design for central Italy, but it is less usual to find the pipes within the central arch themselves divided into three pyramidal arrangements instead of one. The pipes in the two upper tiers, normally also arranged in pyramid form, are here disposed perhaps so as to suggest a pair of small positives. The retaining framework of the central arch is itself again based on ancient classical forms, and at the head of each section hangs a small carved musical trophy. Above the two outer ones may be seen carvings of miniature three-rung ladders, repeated on the cornice; these are references to the 'scala' in the title of the church.

SIENA   Palazzo Pubblico (Cappella)

209   A small organ based on 4-foot pipe-tone only but which seems rather too large to qualify for the description of 'positive', which is nevertheless sometimes applied to it. On the other hand it presents the appearance of being rather larger than it actually is; this is because the design

of the case and arrangment of the display pipes is the exact pattern of that followed in many much larger Italian organs (see e.g. 214, 215, 218–219, 222). The instrument, like that in Santa Maria della Scala (208), was made by Giovanni di Antonio Piffaro, 1519–23, the case being the work of Giovanni di Pietro Castelnuovo. The text-book Renaissance ornament is in gold against a background of blue and black. The panel below the impost, painted with a series of heraldic devices, dates from a restoration of 1635.

FIRENZE   Santissima Annunziata

The Epistle organ, case 1523 by Giovanni d'Alessio, instrument by Domenico di Lorenzo of 210
Lucca. The design is the same as that in Santa Maria della Scala (208), except that the roundels and upper tiers of small pipes have been transposed, the latter in the more usual pyramidal arrangement, and the cornice is topped by a broken pediment with central cartouche.

MODENA   San Pietro

The inscription on the impost states that the organ was completed in 1524 by Giovanni 211
Battista Facchetti of Brescia. Painted wings were supplied by Giulio and Giovanni Taraschi, who also painted the gallery. These wings have now been replaced as part of a restoration in the 1960s which took place after this photograph was taken, and which has made the arrangement of the front more intelligible. The use of three-dimensional figures at this period is unusual. The display pipes are original.

BOLOGNA   San Michele in Bosco

Also by Facchetti of Brescia, begun 1524, the front arranged in a form that he favoured (see 212
also 214). The engaged columns at the sides are an unusual feature. In 1724 alterations were made by Giovanni Francesco Traeri, including the installation of new display pipes, and the style of the pipe shades and other ornament within the display front indicate that Traeri provided these also.

BRESCIA   Duomo Vecchio

Built 1536–7 by Gian Giacomo Antegnati, the case constructed by Bartolomeo Piantavigna 213
and wings (now displayed elsewhere in the cathedral) painted by Girolamo Romanino. The front is planned in the manner of Facchetti, and the entire case is reminscent of an altar tabernacle. In 1824 the Bergamo firm of Serassi added pedal pipes but managed to conceal them satisfactorily behind two canvas-covered wings which can be detected at each side of the case.

GENOVA   Cattedrale di San Lorenzo

Another organ originally by Facchetti of Brescia, 1552, in his favourite arrangement. The 214
framework of the display flat, with its volute-style pediment, is more elaborate than usual, and the wings were competently painted by Andrea Ansoldo da Voltri.

BOLOGNA   San Martino

By Giovanni Cipri of Ferrara, completed 1556, carving by Giacomo Marcovaldi of Bologna. 215
A case showing some affinity with those of d'Alessi at Florence (210), allowing for the transposition of the outer compartments with those next to them.

VERONA   Sant'Anastasia

Restored in 1560 by Giovanni Cipri, who undoubtedly altered the case to suit his own design 216
and was assisted in this by Andrea Scudellino the carver. Here the whole display front, not

just the central arch as at Bologna (215), is contained within the round arch. The upper tier of dummy pipes in the central section is not sufficiently visually emphatic to make any significant contribution to the general design. Floating angelic figures are found on the spandrels of the main arch just as at Bologna, but the winged harpies and grinning satyrs (retainers of the large pipes) are vivid comments on the entry of Renaissance secularism within the very walls of the Church.

MILANO   Santa Maria della Passione

217-20 Epistle and Gospel organs in virtually identical cases, seen, as they should be, in a single *coup d'œil* (218-9). The 1558 Epistle organ (217) was built originally by Gian Giacomo Antegnati and has wings finely painted with scenes from the Passion by Carlo Urbino of Crema; on the pediment is carved a three-dimensional figure of God the Father. The 1613 Gospel organ (220) has wings painted on the same theme by Daniele Crispi and has a figure of Our Lady of the Passion (or the Seven Sorrows) on the pediment. A close inspection will reveal that the display pipes of the Epistle organ are modern (1918) replacements whose mouths are of a different shape to the original ones in the Gospel organ.

ORVIETO   Duomo

221 Case designed 1582 by the architect Ippolito Scalza, not all of whose ideas (including the supporting of the gallery on columns) were put into practice, either for the organ or indeed for the rest of the cathedral, on which he was also long employed. However, the case, as eventually completed to house an instrument by Domenico Benvenuti of Rome, is sufficiently monumental. The design derives ultimately from the form used by Domenico di Lorenzo (see 210), but the massive superstructure and figures above the front pediment are a new and unusual departure in Italy.

BOLOGNA   San Petronio

222, 223 In 1686 the Gospel organ was rehoused, as was also the Epistle organ (205, 206). The arrangement of its fronts, however, is in an earlier style and dates back to alterations of 1641 which in turn had been made to the original organ of 1596 by Baldassare Malamini. The present arrangement of the display pipes probably approximates to the original appearance of the Epistle organ.

ROMA   San Giovanni in Laterano

224 Case by Giovanni Battista Montano of Milan, dated 1598, organ by Luca Blasi. This is a late Renaissance work verging on the Baroque, the main display front contained within a single arch and the complete front elongated to a degree unusual in Italian organs, by the simple means of adding on wings which are basically repetitions of the central section, though reverting to the usual three-arched arrangement. The central pipe in each division is spirally embossed.

QUINZANO   San Rocco

225 Attributed to Costanzo Antegnati, *c.* 1600, and thought to have come from a monastery at Quinzano suppressed in 1810. Certainly the ornate case and gallery were not originally designed for this comparatively small church, and many details of the instrument's construction and tonal qualities point to the Antegnati. Apart from the ornament the arrangement of pipes is in the simplest tripartite arrangement which looks back to San Pietro at Perugia (207).

LUCCA Duomo

The Gospel organ, case carved 1615 by Sante Landucci for an instrument by Andrea and   226
Cosimo Ravani. A simple box case with wings, but unusual in the very narrow compartments
and the equal heights of all the arched compartment heads. The absence of retaining bars in
front of each pipe rank is also unusual but is presumably a fairly modern innovation perhaps
dating from a restoration in 1962. The gallery parapet is especially beautiful.

BOLOGNA San Salvatore

One of a pair of identical cases that stand against the east walls of the transepts; they date   227
from 1620-1, when they originally contained organs by Vincenzo Colonna of Venice and his
adopted son Antonio dal Corno of Brescia, who set up their joint workshop in Bologna. The
simple arrangement of the front might, one feels, have been marginally improved by the
addition of small pipe compartments above the two existing outer ones; such a design would
still have kept within traditional lines and avoided the feeling of too much space in these two
areas.

PESARO Oratorio del Santissimo Nome di Dio

A small case of c. 1625 whose Baroque affinities are revealed in the slightly convex shape of the   228
front, the large terms at the head of the dividing verticals, the urns above the cornice and
panels of 'memento mori' below the pipe feet. The front retaining bars also have now developed
into fully fledged cherubs.

ROMA Santa Maria della Pace

A case of c. 1650 housing an instrument first placed in the church in 1507. The design of three   229
self-contained though linked display units, though also found elsewhere in this part of Italy as
well as in Rome itself, is here rendered unsatisfactory by the fussy and indeed ugly decoration.

ROMA Santa Maria in Vallicella

One of two mid-seventeenth-century Baroque cases standing in the transepts of this church   230
(this shows the Gospel side). The designer has at last achieved total freedom—under the
influence of Baroque thought—from the architectural restrictions of tradition, and has thrown
these to the winds—perhaps the same winds that agitate the draperies of the angels perched
midway up the verticals. Yet it could be said that these same angels and the exuberant
cartouche they support between them are direct descendants of the old front retaining bar.
The spirally-embossed display pipes are an important decorative feature.

GENOVA Santa Maria Assunta di Carignano

A glance at this case should indicate that its origins are not Italian. This is confirmed by the   231
outline of the front with its three main towers, the front plan of UVUVUVU (with no intervening flats—an unusual circumstance in any design), French-style turrets on the end towers,
folding shutters, and carved figures on top of the case. In fact it was designed by Georg
Heigenmann, presumably a German, for the Flemish organ builder Willem Hermans, and
was built 1657–60 with the aid of Italian craftsmen. The shutters were painted by Paolo
Brozzi and Domenico Piola.

Having said this, however, it is worth noting that, were the area between the two end
towers flat instead of U- and V-shaped, the actual arrangement of pipes would be the same as
that in numerous Italian organs of traditional design, such as those at Siena (209), Bologna
(212), Brescia (213), Genova cathedral (214), Milan (218–9), Ardesio (238), and many others.
Nor do the pipe shades conceal the tops of the pipes as they would do in northern Europe.

PISTOIA   Spirito Santo

232   Another instrument (1669) by Willem Hermans, on the north wall of the nave and faced by an imitation front on the south. Although this Baroque case is in its general appearance plainly North European, there is some slight concession to Italian style in that the front, though not flat, is only very slightly convex and the pipes are arranged in pyramid formation with their tops not reaching the shades. However, they have no retaining bars and in the two end compartments the feet rest on shallow v-shaped toe boards. On the other side of the shutters is painted a reproduction of the actual front. The explanation for this apparently pointless exercise is perhaps the desire to keep the appearance of the organ during penitential seasons when it would be temporarily out of liturgical use.

BOLOGNA   SS Gregorio e Siro

233   The Gospel organ, 1673, by Carlo Traeri, the design unusual only in the unpleasantly wide spacing of the smaller display pipes (probably a modern development) and the curiously-shaped top.

SAN SEVERINO MARCHE   San Severino al Monte

234   Despite its basically simple Italianate design, this heavily ornamented case was the work of the Frenchman Dominique Pulvier, and indeed the decoration contains elements of mid-seventeenth-century French Baroque taste, such as the foliated arabesques of the pipe shades, the seraphim, and the frond-like support bar of the central compartment. The instrument, however, was built 1673 by Giuseppe Catarinozzi of Rome. Spirally-embossed display pipes (the centre one in each group) are found here as at Santa Maria in Vallicella and San Giovanni in Laterano, Rome (224, 230).

BURGUSIO   Chiesa parrochiale

235   This organ, brought to Burgusio in 1807 from the nearby monastery of Marienberg, was built 1677–8 by Carlo Prati of Trent. The case is a product of the cultural melting-pot arising from the inevitable fusion in this area of Italian and German traditions. An Italian front is framed in an elaborately carved Baroque tabernacle, with columns in the 'barley sugar twist' form so beloved of the Baroque, side-pieces that recall the organs of North Europe, and large carved figures, those of the trumpet-playing angels in front clinging to the broken pediment as though about to slide off onto the floor at any moment.

NAPOLI   San Gregorio Armeno

236, 237   The mid-seventeenth-century Gospel and Epistle organs, in which a typically Neopolitan Baroque enthusiasm finally overcomes classical decorum except in the matter of the actual arrangement of display pipes and the retention—though in a much more elaborate form—of the front retaining bars. Apart from these clues there would be little visual evidence to link these cases with Italian tradition.

ARDESIO   Santuario della Madonna delle Grazie

238   This later seventeenth-century case gives the lie to the facile assumption that Italian organ cases of the Baroque period cannot rival those of North Europe in the vivacity and luxuriance of their decoration. This is perhaps especially true of cases in Upper Lombardy and more especially of those designed and worked by members of the woodcarving family of the Fantoni of Rovetta in Bergamo, whose archives still contain a large number of designs for organ cases made over a long period of time. The case here at Ardesio was designed by the most famous of the Fantoni, Andrea (1695–1734), who has left the traditional arrangement of the front alone whilst concentrating all his energies on the overall decoration.

GANDINO   Santa Maria Assunta

A sketch which appears to be a design for this florid Baroque case (part of which consists of   239
trompe l'œil painting) has been found amongst the archives of the Fantoni (see 238). The
apology for a *Positivo*, which is stuffed into the central panel of the gallery parapet, suggests
that the Fantoni, whilst attracted to the idea in principle, did not understand either the
function or the historical background of this division of the organ.

GROSOTTO   Santuario della Beata Vergine delle Grazie

A late Baroque case of great virtuosity, begun 1706 by Paolo Scabrini and completed 1713 by   240
Giovanni Battista Dal Piaz. The instrument housed in this epitome of the Italian carver's art
was by Giovanni Battista Raina of Como, enlarged by his son Giuseppe in 1730.

REZZATO   Santa Maria in Valverde

Organ built in 1716 by Giuseppe Bonatti. The normal proportions of this rich Baroque front   241
have been extended by the addition of two concave-fronted compartments at the ends of the
case, and the contours of the front itself rendered more interesting by the addition of free-
standing ornamental columns. If there is a prototype for the main front it could be said to
exist in the organs of Santa Maria della Passione at Milan (217–220), particularly in the
raising up above the normal foot level of the lower compartments in the double tiers; this is
unusual in Italian organs (though also found at Milan). The device of a painting housed in a
separate tabernacle frame raised above the main cornice is an Italian tradition found also in,
for example, San Salvatore at Bologna (227).

VERONA   San Tommaso Cantuariense

Another organ by Bonatti, also built in 1716 (see 241), although the Baroque fripperies of the   242
Rezzato case have been severely pruned. Unusual features are the absence of a central single-
tier compartment of large display pipes and the prominence of the tabernacle frame in the
pediment, on which are displayed the arms of the Saibante family. On this organ, and a
sixteenth-century one (of which the case alone now survives) facing it on the end wall of the
south transept, Mozart and his father gave a joint recital on 7 January 1770. The rare dedication of the church to St Thomas à Becket should not go unnoticed.

L'AQUILA   San Bernardino

An anonymous instrument in a Baroque case of *c.* 1725, carved by Bernardino Mosca of   243
Pescocostanzo. The basic design of the front could be said to be a variation on that of Rezzato
(241), though incorporating 'barley sugar twist' pillars instead of classical ones. The arrangement of pipes within the central flat, though less usual, is found elsewhere in Italy (see also
244, 247, 248). Especially striking is the great cartouche-cum-pipe-shade device in the central
compartment which links the decorative elements below the cornice to those above it.

BOLOGNA   San Domenico

This charming eighteenth-century organ is found on the Epistle side of the Cappella del   244
Rosario in the church, faced on the Gospel side by a dummy replica. Although some of the
scrolled decoration contains elements of the Rococo, the case as a whole is assimilated into the
surrounding painted architectural setting in the assured illusionistic manner typical of the
Baroque era at its best, the flower paintings being especially fine. The arrangement of pipes is
the same as that at L'Aquila (243), though here presenting a single flat only. The pipe shades
are also of the same type.

UDINE   Duomo

245   The Gospel organ, now basically an eighteenth-century instrument in an earlier case, thought
to be that of an organ built 1549–50 by Vincenzo Colombi of Venice. If this is so, it suggests a
case originally like that in the cathedral at Lucca (226), though not in the arrangement of
display pipes for which other precedents may easily be found. The original case has certainly
had Baroque details added to it, such as the carved side-pieces replacing shutters which are
known to have been painted 1553–5 by Pomponio Amalteo.

VENEZIA   San Giorgio Maggiore

246   A mainly architectural composition which looks less like an organ case than a stone screen in
which organ pipes have been placed almost as an afterthought. The instrument it houses is of
the mid-eighteenth century but the case is somewhat older. It stands above the screen
dividing the sanctuary and retrochoir from the body of the church and is a rare if not unique
example of an Italian organ so situated (i.e. on a screen). The thin carvings of musical instruments which act as apologies for pipe shades in the central compartments, the musical putti
and the angels on the pediment seem ill-proportioned both in respect of each other and of the
case itself; one suspects that they are all later additions.

FANO   San Paterniano

247   A square tabernacle-type case of 1775 housing an instrument by Gaetano Callido. The
decoration is strictly classical; in particular the trophies of muscial instruments in the
spandrels of the arch recall the Renaissance. The wide-span single arch and the distinctive
arrangement of pipes already seen at L'Aquila and Bologna (243, 244) typify the Venetian
school at this period (see also 248).

VENEZIA   San Raffaele Arcangelo

248   This Rococo *jeu d'esprit* of 1749 makes a cheerful if untypical note on which to end the Italian
survey. The original instrument was by Gaetano Amigazzi of Verona.

British Isles

OLD RADNOR   St Stephen

This anonymous case is always assumed to date in essentials from somewhere between 1500 **249** and 1550, though it was restored in 1872 under the guidance of the Rev. F. H. Sutton, an antiquary who made the study of organ cases and the restoration of ancient ones his especial province. The case at Old Radnor cannot be compared with other British cases of similar date and appearance, since none exist. It bears no resemblance to those surviving British cases which appear to be next to it in date, i.e. those at St Lawrence, Appleby (*c.* 1570) and Gloucester cathedral (*Chaire* case, *c.* 1580). The V-shaped towers in combination with double-tiered flats give it a Continental appearance. Sutton published a monograph about it (*Some account of the medieval organ case still existing at Old Radnor, South Wales*, 1866), in which a drawing shows the organ case before restoration looking substantially the same as it does today. Yet somehow, both then and now, it fails to be entirely convincing, mainly perhaps because a continuous cornice uninterrupted by towers or pinnacles is not a normal feature of Gothic and/or Renaissance organ cases anywhere else in North Europe. Furthermore he would be a bold man who would assign to the rather ponderously carved half-circles and other decorative details a specific sixteenth-century date. Possibly therefore the organ's appearance had already been altered at least once before Sutton's restoration. His judgement was by no means infallible, as is shown by his solecism of inserting vertically-conceived linenfold panelling *horizontally* as part of his restoration programme.

TEWKESBURY   Abbey Church

This, the so-called 'Milton' organ, originally stood somewhere in Magdalen College, Oxford **250** (probably in the chapel). Soon after 1654 it was removed to Hampton Court for the delectation of Oliver Cromwell. John Milton was Cromwell's secretary as well as an accomplished musician and there is therefore an almost inevitable though not entirely improbable tradition that he played this organ for his master; hence its name. At the Restoration in 1660 the organ was returned to Magdalen College where it remained until sold to Tewkesbury in 1737. Its present position (south side of the choir) is one of several that it has occupied in the Abbey since its first arrival there.

Its date cannot be precisely determined and it has without doubt undergone changes. However, the late Renaissance style of the decoration and of the arcading below the impost indicates a date somewhere in the late sixteenth or early seventeenth century; this would be consistent with the theory held by some experts that the case originally housed an instrument provided for the College in 1597 by John Chappington. The embossed pipes are a valuable original survival, and the shades are stepped on Continental lines. A five-tower front is a rarity in English organ cases; after the Restoration the almost universal preference was for three towers, and of the few extant cases from pre-1660 this is the only example having five. Even here the two thin inner towers of only three pipes each are so tentative and vestigial as to suggest that the designer was uncertain whether to include them or not.

The case is double-fronted, but the secondary front is an uninteresting design which dates probably from the eighteenth century.

CAMBRIDGE   King's College Chapel

251   A justly-famed double-fronted case of great beauty; this plate shows the east front. The instrument, which stands on the Renaissance screen at the entrance to the main body of the chapel, was made 1605–6 and the main case constructed for the organ builder, Thomas Dallam, by the firm of Chapman and Hartop of Cambridge. A *Chaire* organ in a well-matched case was provided later (1661) by Lancelot Pease. Removed during the Commonwealth period and re-erected on the screen at the Restoration, the most significant of subsequent alterations to the instrument were probably those of Renatus Harris in 1688, but there is no reason to suppose that Harris altered the general appearance of the case to any great extent. The Dallam family used this form of a curving cornice sweeping upwards to culminate in two end towers on at least three other occasions—at St George's Chapel, Windsor, and in Brittany at Quimper and Saint-Pol-de-Léon (where Thomas's son Robert became organist of the cathedral). Various rebuilds have made the case much deeper than it originally was, but this has not affected the proportions of the two fronts.

Though the excellent proportions and graceful, sweeping outlines of this case are its chief claim to visual beauty, the typical, crisply-carved Renaissance figures, grotesques and arabesques also make a significant contribution to the total effect. The crowns (a reference to the royal foundation of the College) and heraldic devices on the tower caps are equally well proportioned.

GLOUCESTER   Cathedral

252   Case and instrument completed 1666 by Thomas Harris. He is said to have used a *Chaire* case from a much older organ of 1579, but the evidence for this is not wholly convincing; if some of the ornament of the *Chaire* organ is Renaissance in character, so also are Harris's columns crowned with arches which form the frames for the main case flats, and for the substructure arches below the two end towers. (The *Chaire* case appears to be similar in design to that provided in 1609 for the organ of St George's Chapel, Windsor, by Harris's father-in-law, Thomas Dallam.) The single tall pipe in the centre of the *Chaire* case is certainly an unusual feature, but Harris could well have found his inspiration for it in Continental sources, since he lived in France during the period of the Commonwealth. Another unusual feature—at least amongst English cases—is that the central tower of the main case, though shorter than the two end ones, is nevertheless raised to the same level; normally it would be either lower (254) or higher (253). The ornamental finial on the central tower of the *Chaire* case is similar in style to those on the towers of the Tewkesbury 'Milton' organ (250); this is perhaps an argument in favour of a sixteenth-century date for the *Chaire* case.

Both the cases at Gloucester are remarkable for the amount of heraldic painting with which the display pipes are decorated, and which was originally executed by John Campion, a local artist. This type of decoration was probably fairly widespread on pre-Commonwealth British organs—it is found, for example, on the late sixteenth-century organ at Framlingham in Suffolk—but was perhaps already something of a decorative anachronism by the time the Gloucester organ was built. At Gloucester the arms shown are mainly those of royalty (Charles II and James, Duke of York) and of the staff and benefactors of the cathedral.

The case is double-fronted, but the west front (not illustrated) is much plainer (except for more painted pipes), since although the organ now stands on the choir screen it was not originally intended to do so, and in fact was sited in a loft on the south side of the choir until transferred to the screen in 1718. 'Gothick' pinnacles were added to it in *c.* 1740 but were removed again during the nineteenth century, probably by Henry Willis.

The photograph shown here was taken before the organ's most recent restoration, completed in 1971. During this, the depth of the main case between the two fronts (much enlarged over the years) was decreased again to something like its original dimension, the additional wooden pedal pipes at the sides (outside the case proper) were removed, the arcading below the impost was opened up, and the whole case was slightly raised.

EXETER Cathedral

Case and instrument by John Loosemore, 1665; double-fronted (the plate shows the east   253
front) and now with two *Chaire* cases, that on the west front being an 1891 reproduction of the
original on the east front.

The circular pipe compartments in the upper flats are rare though not unique in English case design, but this is perhaps the earliest extant example of them. They have in fact an un-English appearance, as have also the three small three-pipe compartments (the upper ones being rounded on plan) between the main flats and the towers.

Also in 1891 the case was raised and made deeper. An 1876 rebuild by Henry Speechly had already involved the melting down of the original gilt and embossed tin display pipes and the removal of two free-standing towers built by Loosemore to harmonise with the case and to contain a set of 'Double Diapason' pipes; these were his answer to the Continental pedal pipes which English organs of the period could not boast.

Loosemore built few organs but was rightly honoured for his work, of which Exeter was without doubt the finest example; it is therefore fitting that he is buried in the cathedral.

ADLINGTON HALL, CHESHIRE

A large and impressive house organ standing in a gallery at one end of a Tudor hall that is   254
part of a private mansion. The carved cartouche above the central tower relates to a family
marriage which took place in 1683, but the organ itself is certainly earlier, perhaps *c.* 1670.
The instrument has been attributed—at least in part—to Bernard Smith, although the lower
section incorporating a most un-English-looking *Brustwerk* is probably older and comes from
some other instrument.

The central tower of a typical Smith three-tower case is normally taller than the two outer ones. On the other hand, a particularly satisfying vertical unity is given to the case by the repetition in both the upper and lower sections of the fluted pilasters at the ends. The carving is rich and of good quality; especially fine are the acanthus *culs-de-lampe* beneath the end towers.

This organ—which was known to Handel, who stayed at the Hall—was finely restored in 1959 after coming dangerously near to complete destruction through total neglect.

LONDON St Paul's Cathedral

Sir Christopher Wren designed this famous case to house the instrument by Bernard Smith,   255
built 1695–6. It was placed on the choir screen, with two identical fronts and a single *Chaire*
case. Wren had actually wanted to site it in one of the choir bays. In addition to being over-
ruled on this point he was obliged to add two altar-like structures, with attendant figures, on
the tops of the towers, in order to conceal Smith's longest bass pipes. Originally the two
fronts were encased in a system of glass shutters, also designed by Wren, whose main purpose
was to keep dust out of the organ's pipes and mechanism; however scientifically desirable and
typical of Wren's inventive mind these shutters may have been, old engravings show that
they were a visual disaster and thankfully they were removed in 1826.

In 1872 the case was divided in two and the identical halves placed in their present positions in the choir. The east front and *Chaire* case were placed on the north side, the west front placed opposite and provided with an exact replica of the original *Chaire* case.

The designer, situation and period of this case all combine to ensure that it is a unique example and stands outside the main traditions of English case design. Nevertheless it is a Baroque *tour-de-force* which owes its impact not only to Wren but to the unrivalled skill of Grinling Gibbons who carved it.

LONDON   The Tower, Chapel of St Peter-ad-Vincula

256   Built 1699 by Bernard Smith for the Banqueting House in Whitehall, which had then been converted into a chapel and remained so until 1890. On the closure of the chapel in that year the organ was transferred to the Tower.

This design of four towers and three flats, U–U–U–U, the inner towers taller than the outer, was a favourite form with Smith, who is known to have used it on at least five other occasions in England. Engravings show that as originally built the upper case overhung the substructure, but this arrangement was lost when the organ was moved to the Tower. The finely-carved, pierced and scrolled pipe shades and toe boards, the tower supports strongly carved with cherubs' heads and acanthus, and the heavy faceted tower caps are all typical not only of Smith but of much seventeenth- and early eighteenth-century English case design in general.

TWICKENHAM   All Hallows

257   Built in 1703 by Smith's rival, Renatus Harris, for All Hallows, Lombard Street, in the City of London. In 1937 the church was declared to be in danger of collapse, and accordingly its furniture and fittings, including the organ, were removed to the somewhat bare modern church of the same name, where they look incongruous and out of place. The organ stands self-consciously in a gallery at the west end.

This case is a departure from the form which Harris seems most to have favoured, consisting basically of the U–U–U plan (he is not known ever to have used four towers) with the intervening flats crowned by convex cornices. Here the cornices are concave, the central tower small and short (with Harris it is usually not only taller than the other two but is continuous from impost level upwards), and the lower tier almost circular. This last is an unusual feature in any organ case, perhaps because the variations in size of the display pipes always look contrived and unsatisfactory. However, the slightly uncomfortable impression conveyed by the general design of this case is more than offset by the wealth of excellent carving which it bears, notably around the circular flat and on the impost, where the central trophy of musical instruments is especially fine.

LONDON   St Magnus the Martyr

258   In 1712 Abraham Jordan, assisted by his son of the same name, supplied this case and instrument. The latter is famous as having been the first English organ into which the principle of a moving Swell shutter was introduced; this was a development of the seventeenth-century *Echo* division in which a selection of solo pipe ranks were permanently enclosed in a box, giving an effect of distance.

In its general appearance this case is nearer to the St Paul's Cathedral organ than to any other English case of the period. However, the introduction of the Swell division prompted the need for new ideas on design, and it is interesting to observe the basic similarity between this case and some Iberian ones, more especially in the feature of a continuous cornice with broken pediment framing a tabernacle superstructure. Something of the kind can be seen in plates 169, 182, 184 and 190—though these are for the most part much more highly ornamented—and it is therefore worth remembering that Jordan is sometimes said to have got his ideas about the Swell division from experiments being conducted on the same lines in both Spain and Portugal. Though few if any English organ builders adopted similar designs for their cases, preferring to conceal the Swell within the body of the instrument, its introduction and general acceptance certainly meant that from Jordan's time onward cases had to be built higher so as to contain it.

The Baroque carving of the St Magnus case—especially the panels of musical instruments beneath the flats—is in the finest tradition of the period.

LONDON St Vedast

Built 1731 by John Harris and the elder John Byfield, originally for the church of St Bartholomew-by-the-Exchange. After removal to two other London churches, in 1841 and 1904 successively, it was finally installed in the rebuilt St Vedast in 1961–3.

Although the three-tower arrangement was usual in England at this period, the beautiful fluid shapes (both in plan and elevation) of the intervening flats are more rare, although several examples are to be found in and around London. The depth of pipe shades is by now considerably decreased.

KING'S LYNN St Margaret

With this organ in its graceful case the immigrant Swiss-born organ builder Johann Snetzler first made his name in England in 1754, at the instigation of Dr Charles Burney, the musicologist and at that time organist of the church. Originally the organ stood in a gallery at the west end of the church, where no doubt it appeared to better advantage than in its present cramped position under an arch at the north side of the chancel. Its proportions are also visually spoiled by the addition of uncased modern pipes at each side.

At the outset of his successful career Snetzler here introduces us to one of the hallmarks of his typical case design, both in chamber and church instruments—the contrary motion of shaped toe boards and pipe mouths as opposed to that of V-shaped pipe shades. There is some restrained reference to the Rococo in the shells and C-scrolls that replace the traditional crowns, mitres or shields on the tower tops, in the pipe shades, and in the central latticework decoration on the toe boards.

LONDON Greenwich Hospital Chapel

Built 1789 by Samuel Green, the case intended to harmonise with the decorations of the chapel which were carried out by James Stuart and William Newton in the Greek Revival style of which Stuart was then the celebrated exponent.

Considered in isolation, the case is an elegant revamping of the old four-tower plan, with incurving flats and recessed central section in which Green makes use of the oval display panel which he especially favoured in his chamber organs. The pipe shades are in the form of the anthemion, or Greek honeysuckle motif, and this is repeated at the level of the impost, continuing the same frieze which appears on the wall of the chapel behind. The same motif is repeated as the crown-like projections on the tower caps, and the Greek key or meander motif is carved at the feet of the tower pipes.

Despite all this, the general design of the case does not differ sufficiently from the traditional to fit convincingly into its Classical background, for which something more strongly architectural in character would perhaps have been better suited.

WYMONDHAM Abbey Church

A fanciful essay in light-hearted eighteenth-century 'Gothick', a decorative style derived from medieval sources but entirely free of the solemn religious note with which the Victorians later invested it. Case and instrument here were built 1793 by James Davis, working for the London music firm of Longman and Broderip. This is a west end gallery siting.

259

260

261

262

LINCOLN Cathedral

263, 264   An early nineteenth-century Gothic case, designed by E. J. Willson for an instrument built 1826 by William Allen. Here the restraint of Davis's case at Wymondham is replaced by a strong desire to cover everything with pinnacles, crockets and ogee arches. This typifies a kind of frenzy that seized many designers of the period, who seem to have felt the increasing solemnities of the Gothic Revival creeping up gradually upon them like a disease; Sir John Sutton (see 66) wrote feelingly in 1847 of 'these unsightly organ cases, which became every day larger and more heavy looking', and compared their decoration to 'the barley sugar ornaments we see about Christmas time in pastry cooks' windows, displayed in all their glory on a Twelfth cake.'

Nevertheless, the Lincoln case is by no means a visual failure, and indeed is not inappropriate in its context. The interesting polygonal *Chaire* case was appended in 1851 by William Allen's son Charles.

Netherlands (North)

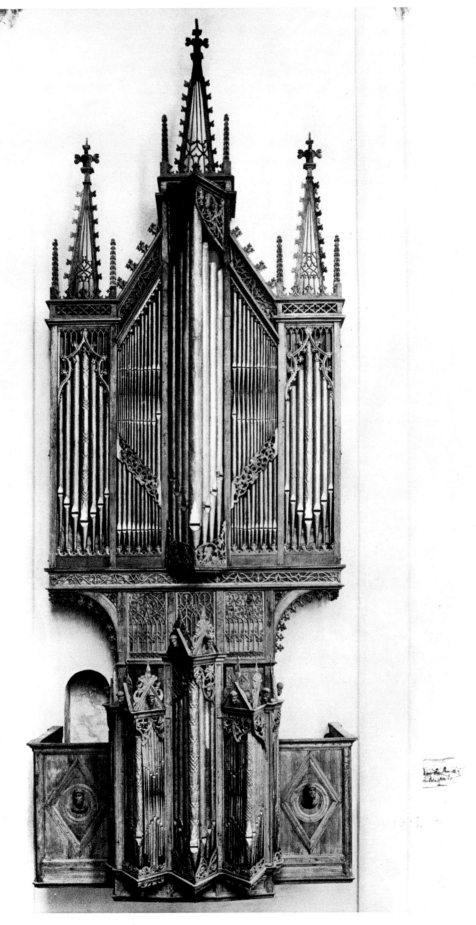

Middelburg (Zeeland), Koorkerk, 1479   I

NETHERLANDS (NORTH)

2   Middelburg (Zeeland), Koorkerk, 1479

NETHERLANDS (NORTH)

Middelburg (Zeeland), Koorkerk, 1479

NETHERLANDS (NORTH)

4   Alkmaar (Noord-Holland), Sint-Laurenskerk, choir organ, 1511

NETHERLANDS (NORTH)

Amsterdam, Rijksmuseum, 1526　　　　5

NETHERLANDS (NORTH)

6   Jutphaas (Utrecht), Sint-Nicolaas, *c.* 1520

NETHERLANDS (NORTH)

Monnikendam (Noord-Holland), Nederlandse Hervormde Kerk, *c.* 1530   7

8   Enkhuizen (Noord-Holland), Sint-Gommaruskerk, 1547

NETHERLANDS (NORTH)

Enkhuizen (Noord-Holland), Sint-Gommaruskerk, 1547

NETHERLANDS (NORTH)

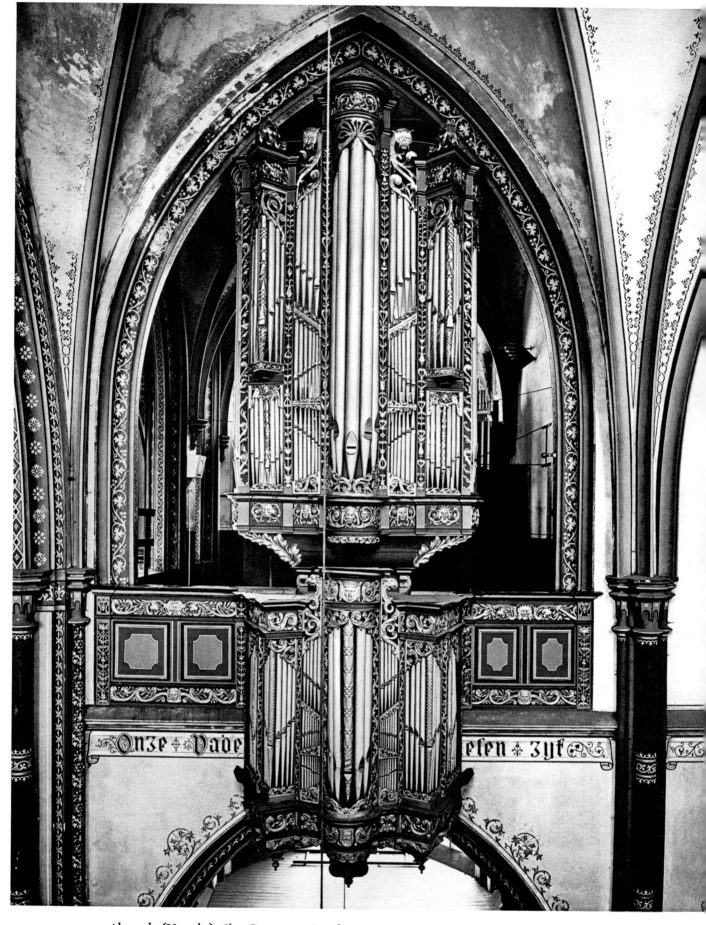

10   Abcoude (Utrecht), Sint-Cosmas-en-Damianus, 1556

NETHERLANDS (NORTH)

Loppersum (Groningen), Nederlandse Hervormde Kerk, 1562   11

12   's-Hertogenbosch (Noord-Brabant), Kathedraal van Sint-Jan, 1618

NETHERLANDS (NORTH)

Alkmaar (Noord-Holland), Sint-Laurenskerk, 1638

NETHERLANDS (NORTH)

14   Zeerijp (Groningen), Nederlandse Hervormde Kerk, 1645

NETHERLANDS (NORTH)

Dordrecht (Zuid-Holland), Onze-Lieve-Vrouwekerk, 1671

15

NETHERLANDS (NORTH)

Medemblik (Noord-Holland), Nederlandse Hervormde Kerk, 1668

NETHERLANDS (NORTH)

Amsterdam, Waalse Kerk, 1680   17

NETHERLANDS (NORTH)

18   Amsterdam, Westerkerk, 1686

NETHERLANDS (NORTH)

Groningen, Martinikerk, 1542

NETHERLANDS (NORTH)

Middelburg (Zeeland), Nieuwe Kerk, 1692

NETHERLANDS (NORTH)

Middelburg (Zeeland), Nieuwe Kerk, 1692

NETHERLANDS (NORTH)

Groningen, A-Kerk, 1699

NETHERLANDS (NORTH)

Culemborg (Gelderland), Sint-Barbarakerk, 1719   23

24   Zwolle (Overijssel), Sint-Michaëlskerk, 1721

NETHERLANDS (NORTH)

's-Gravenhage (Zuid-Holland), Oud-Katholieke Kerk, 1724   25

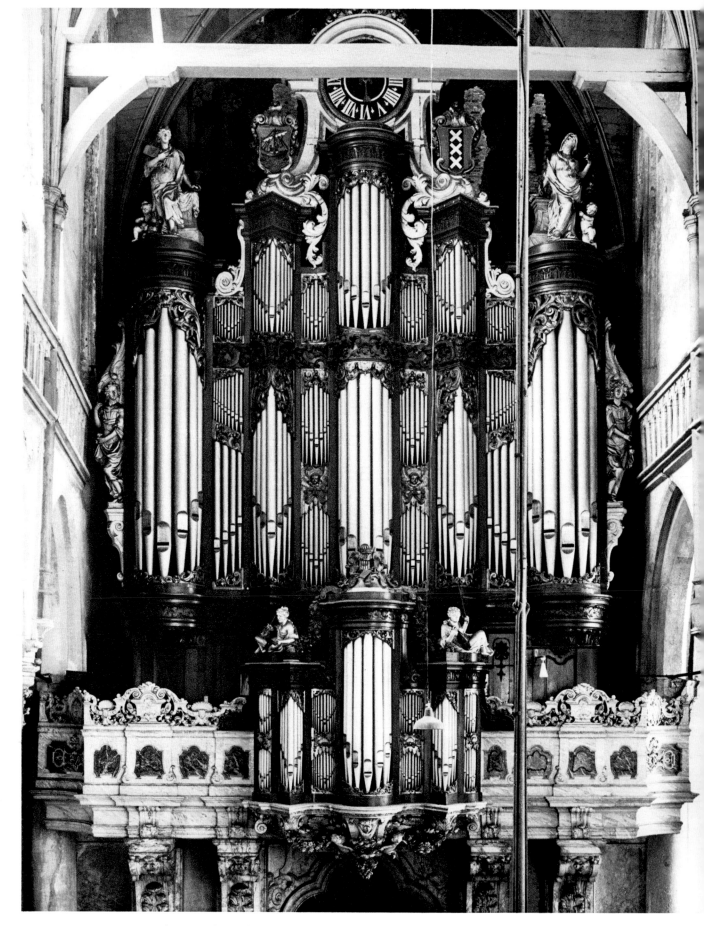

26 Amsterdam, Oude Kerk, 1726

NETHERLANDS (NORTH)

Leens (Groningen), Nederlandse Hervormde Kerk, *c.* 1735

NETHERLANDS (NORTH)

28   Gouda (Zuid-Holland), Sint-Janskerk, 1732

NETHERLANDS (NORTH)

Haarlem (Noord-Holland), Sint-Bavokerk, 1735

30   Teeffelen (Noord-Brabant), Sint-Benedictus, *c.* 1750

Nijkerk (Gelderland), Nederlandse Hervormde Kerk, 1756

NETHERLANDS (NORTH)

's-Gravenhage, Morgensternkerk, *c.* 1740

NETHERLANDS (NORTH)

Helmond (Noord-Brabant), Sint-Lambertus, 1771

33

34   Schiedam (Zuid-Holland), Stedelijk Museum, 1773

NETHERLANDS (NORTH)

Amsterdam, Sint-Franciscus-van-Assisië, *c.* 1775

NETHERLANDS (NORTH)

36 Leiderdorp (Zuid-Holland), Nederlandse Hervormde Kerk, 1781

NETHERLANDS (NORTH)

Bolsward (Friesland), Martinikerk, *c.* 1775

NETHERLANDS (NORTH)

Amsterdam, Stichting Amstelhof, *c.* 1825

NETHERLANDS (NORTH)

Elburg (Gelderland), Nederlandse Hervormde Kerk, 1825

NETHERLANDS (NORTH)

Boxtel (Noord-Brabant), Sint-Petrus, 1842

NETHERLANDS (NORTH)

Schijndel (Noord-Brabant), Sint-Serviatus, 1839   41

42   Naarden (Noord-Holland), Sint-Vituskerk, 1862

NETHERLANDS (NORTH)

Netherlands (South)

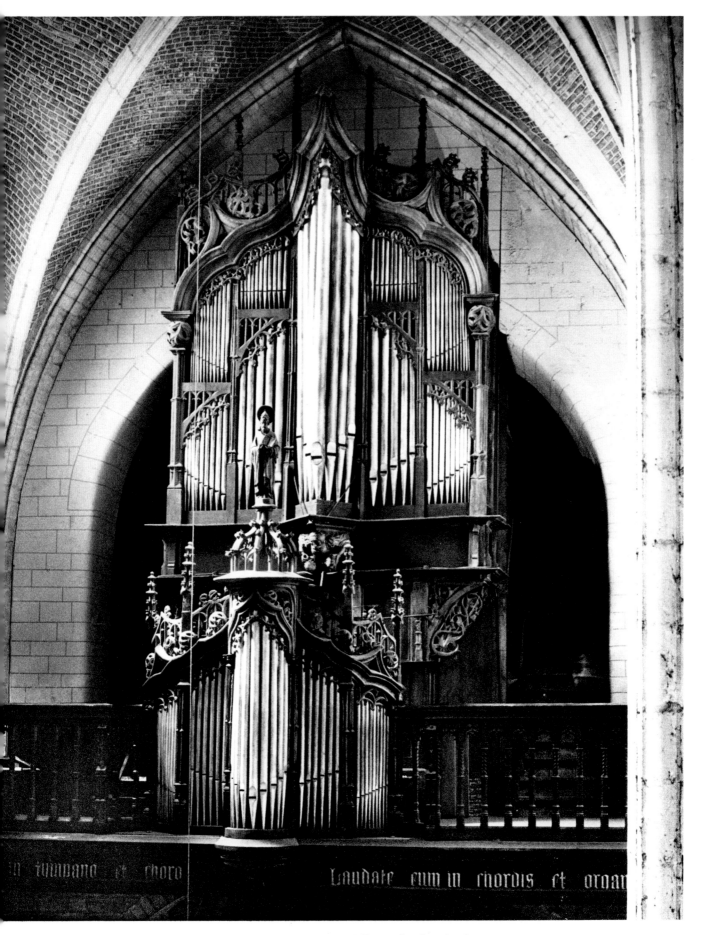

Tienen (Brabant), Sint-Germanus, *c.* 1516

NETHERLANDS (SOUTH)

44   Quenast (Brabant), Saint-Martin, 1540

NETHERLANDS (SOUTH)

Liège, Saint-Denis, 1589　　　45

NETHERLANDS (SOUTH)

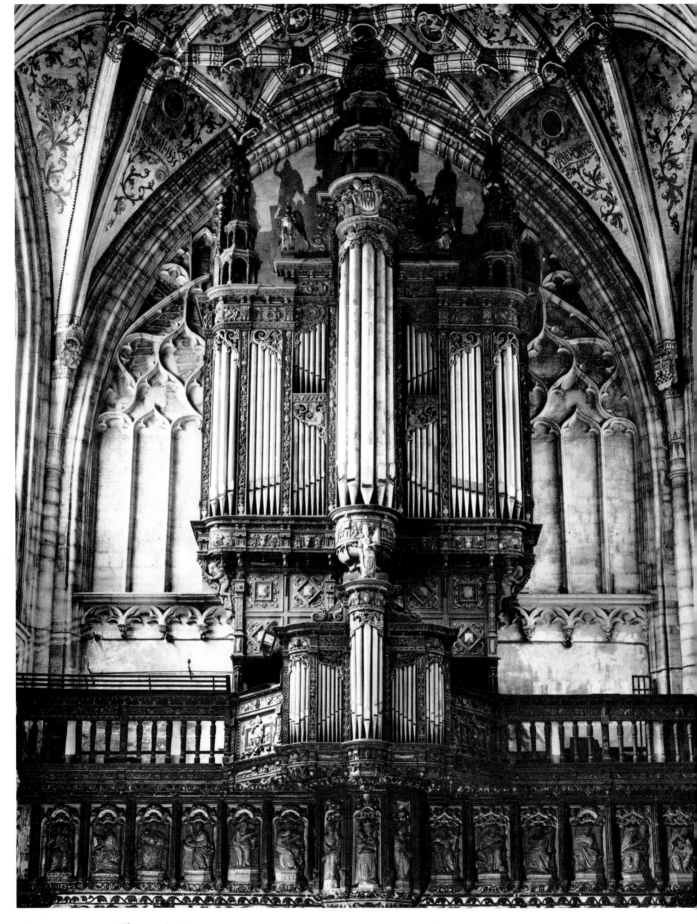

46   Liège, Saint-Jacques, 1600

NETHERLANDS (SOUTH)

Lier (Antwerp), Sint-Gummarus, 1628

NETHERLANDS (SOUTH)

48   Watervliet (Oost-Vlaanderen), Onze-Lieve-Vrouw-Hemelvaart, 1643

NETHERLANDS (SOUTH)

Lissewege (West-Vlaanderen), Onze-Lieve-Vrouw, 1653

NETHERLANDS (SOUTH)

Gent (Oost-Vlaanderen), Sint-Baafskathedraal, 1653

NETHERLANDS (SOUTH)

Antwerp, Sint-Paulus, 1648   51

NETHERLANDS (SOUTH)

52   Mechlin (Antwerp), Onze-Lieve-Vrouw-over-de-Dijle, 1665

NETHERLANDS (SOUTH)

Saint-Hubert (Luxembourg), Basilique Saint-Hubert, 1685

NETHERLANDS (SOUTH)

Stalhille (West-Vlaanderen), Sint-Jan-Baptist, 1715

NETHERLANDS (SOUTH)

Bruges (West-Vlaanderen), Sint-Salvatorkathedraal, 1717 55

56   Antwerp, Sint-Carolus, *c.* 1720

NETHERLANDS (SOUTH)

Antwerp, Sint-Jacob, 1727   57

NETHERLANDS (SOUTH)

58   Tournai (Hainaut), Saint-Jacques, 1753

NETHERLANDS (SOUTH)

Tongeren (Limburg), Onze-Lieve-Vrouw, *c.* 1750

NETHERLANDS (SOUTH)

60 Poperinge (West-Vlaanderen), Onze-Lieve-Vrouw, *c.* 1760

NETHERLANDS (SOUTH)

Mechlin (Antwerp), Sint-Jan, 1759   61

Haringe (West-Vlaanderen), Sint-Martinus, 1778

NETHERLANDS (SOUTH)

Belsele (Oost-Vlaanderen), Sint-Andries-en-Ghislanus, 1784

NETHERLANDS (SOUTH)

Averbode (Brabant), Abdij, 1853

NETHERLANDS (SOUTH)

Austria, Germany, Switzerland

Sion (Valais, sw), Notre-Dame-de-Valère, *c.* 1400　65

66   Kiedrich (Hessen, G), Sankt Valentin, *c.* 1495

AUSTRIA, GERMANY, SWITZERLAND

Lübeck (Schleswig-Holstein, G), Sankt Jakobi, small organ, *c.* 1500

AUSTRIA, GERMANY, SWITZERLAND

68   Innsbruck (Tirol, A), Silberne Kapelle, *c.* 1550

AUSTRIA, GERMANY, SWITZERLAND

Augsburg (Bayern, G), Sankt Anna, Fuggerkapelle, *c.* 1512 (reconstructed)

70   Konstanz (Baden-Württemberg, G), Münster, 1516

AUSTRIA, GERMANY, SWITZERLAND

Nördlingen (Bayern, G), Sankt Georg, 1466   71

AUSTRIA, GERMANY, SWITZERLAND

Klosterneuburg (Niederösterreich, A), Stiftskirche, 1642

AUSTRIA, GERMANY, SWITZERLAND

Stade (Niedersachsen, G), Sankt Cosmae-et-Damiani, 1669   73

74   Corvey (Nordrhein-Westfalen, G), Klosterkirche, 1681

Neuenfelde (Hamburg, G), Sankt Pankrattii, 1688

Landshut (Bayern, G), Sankt Martin, 1700

AUSTRIA, GERMANY, SWITZERLAND

Sankt Urban (Luzern, sw), Klosterkirche, 1716

AUSTRIA, GERMANY, SWITZERLAND

78   Innsbruck (Tirol, A), Sankt Jakob, 1725

AUSTRIA, GERMANY, SWITZERLAND

Ochsenhausen (Baden-Württemberg, G), Klosterkirche, 1729   79

80   Borgentreich (Nordrhein-Westfalen, G), Sankt Johannis Baptist, 1730

Sankt Peter (Baden-Württemberg, G), Klosterkirche, 1732

Melk (Niederösterreich, A), Stiftskirche, 1732

AUSTRIA, GERMANY, SWITZERLAND

Weingarten (Baden-Württemberg, G), Klosterkirche, 1737

AUSTRIA, GERMANY, SWITZERLAND

Weingarten (Baden-Württemberg, G), Klosterkirche, 1737

AUSTRIA, GERMANY, SWITZERLAND

Weingarten (Baden-Württemberg, G), Klosterkirche, 1737   85

Rottenbuch (Bayern, G), Mariä-Geburt-Kirche, 1747

AUSTRIA, GERMANY, SWITZERLAND

Marienfeld (Nordrhein-Westfalen, G), Klosterkirche, 1751 87

88   Einsiedeln (Schwyz, SW), Klosterkirche, 1751

AUSTRIA, GERMANY, SWITZERLAND

Esslingen (Baden-Württemberg, G), Sankt Dionysius, 1706 89

90   Irsee (Bayern, G), Klosterkirche, 1754

Die Wies (Bayern, G), Wallfahrtskirche, c. 1756

91

Ottobeuren (Bayern, G), Klosterkirche, Holy Ghost organ, 1764

AUSTRIA, GERMANY, SWITZERLAND

Ottobeuren, Trinity organ

AUSTRIA, GERMANY, SWITZERLAND

94   Ottobeuren, Holy Ghost organ

Roggenburg (Bayern, G), Stiftskirche, 1752

AUSTRIA, GERMANY, SWITZERLAND

96   Arlesheim (Baselland, sw), Dom, 1759

Fischingen (Thurgau, sw), Klosterkirche, 1763 97

98 Ettal (Bayern, G), Klosterkirche, 1763

AUSTRIA, GERMANY, SWITZERLAND

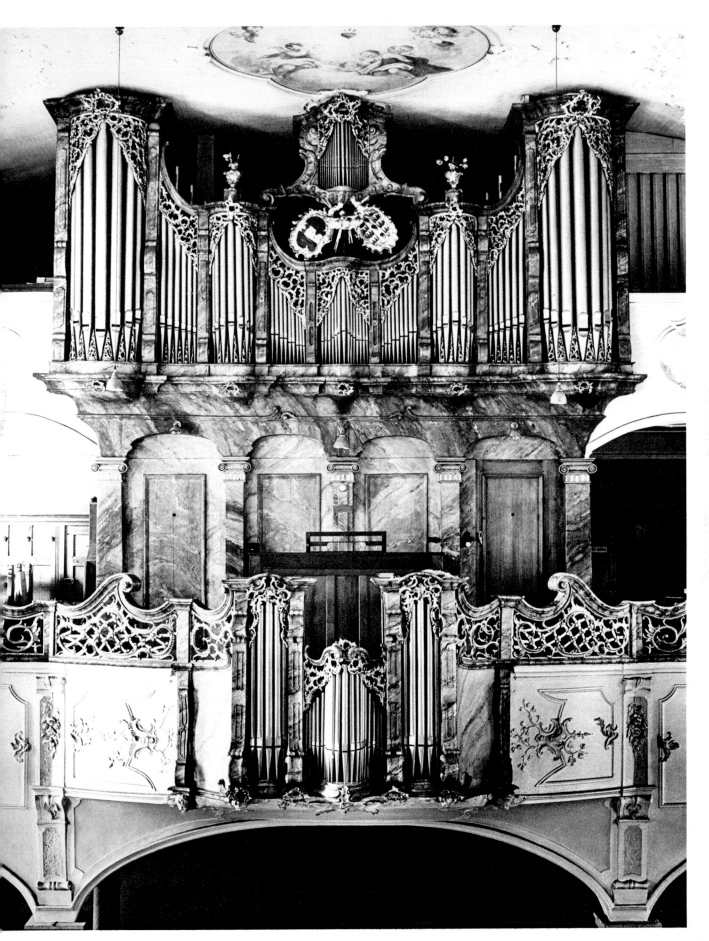

Bregenz (Vorarlberg, A), Sankt Gallus, 1771   99

100   Hilzingen (Baden-Württemberg, G), Sankt Peter-und-Paul, *c.* 1770

AUSTRIA, GERMANY, SWITZERLAND

Salem (Baden-Württemberg, G), Klosterkirche, 1770

AUSTRIA, GERMANY, SWITZERLAND

102   Steingaden (Bayern, G), Klosterkirche, 1743

AUSTRIA, GERMANY, SWITZERLAND

Amorbach (Bayern, G), Abteikirche, 1774   103

AUSTRIA, GERMANY, SWITZERLAND

104 Einsiedeln (Schwyz, sw), Klosterkirche, Gospel organ, 1749

AUSTRIA, GERMANY, SWITZERLAND

Einsiedeln, Epistle organ

AUSTRIA, GERMANY, SWITZERLAND

Sankt Florian (Oberösterreich, A), Stiftskirche, 1770

AUSTRIA, GERMANY, SWITZERLAND

Schwyz (sw), Sankt Martin, 1778   107

AUSTRIA, GERMANY, SWITZERLAND

108   Neresheim (Baden-Württemberg, G), Klosterkirche, 1797

Hof-an-der-Saale (Bayern, G), Sankt Michaelis, 1834

AUSTRIA, GERMANY, SWITZERLAND

Giengen-an-der-Brenz (Baden-Württemberg, G), Sankt Marien, 1905

AUSTRIA, GERMANY, SWITZERLAND

Denmark

Sorø (Sjaelland), Klosterkirke, *c.* 1550   111

112   Roskilde (Sjaelland), Domkirke, 1555

DENMARK

Hillerød (Sjaelland), Frederiksborg Slotskirke, Compenius organ, 1610

113

DENMARK

114   Hillerød, Frederiksborg Slotskirke, Lorenz organ, 1614 (reconstructed)

DENMARK

Haderslev (Jylland), Domkirke, 1652   115

116   København, Vor Frelsers Kirke, 1698

DENMARK

København, Holmens Kirke, 1740   117

DENMARK

118   Odense (Fyn), Domkirke, 1752

DENMARK

France

Strasbourg (Bas-Rhin), Cathédrale Notre-Dame, 1489   119

120   Perpignan (Pyrénées-Orientales), Cathédrale Saint-Jean, *c.* 1500

FRANCE

Amiens (Somme), Cathédrale Notre-Dame, 1549   121

FRANCE

122   Tours (Indre-et-Loire), Cathédrale Saint-Gatien, 1562

FRANCE

La Ferté-Bernard (Sarthe), Notre-Dame-des-Marais, 1536   123

FRANCE

124   Saint-Bertrand-de-Comminges (Haute-Garonne), Cathédrale Notre-Dame, 1536

FRANCE

Caudebec-en-Caux (Seine-Maritime), Notre-Dame, 1542   125

FRANCE

126   Chartres (Eure-et-Loire), Cathédrale Notre-Dame, 1542

FRANCE

Les Andelys (Eure), Notre-Dame du Grand-Andely, 1573 127

FRANCE

128   Rodez (Aveyron), Cathédrale Notre-Dame, 1628

FRANCE

Toulouse (Haute-Garonne), Cathédrale Saint-Étienne, *c.* 1611

129

FRANCE

130 Embrun (Hautes-Alpes), Notre-Dame, 1463

FRANCE

Rouen (Seine-Maritime), Saint-Ouen, 1630   131

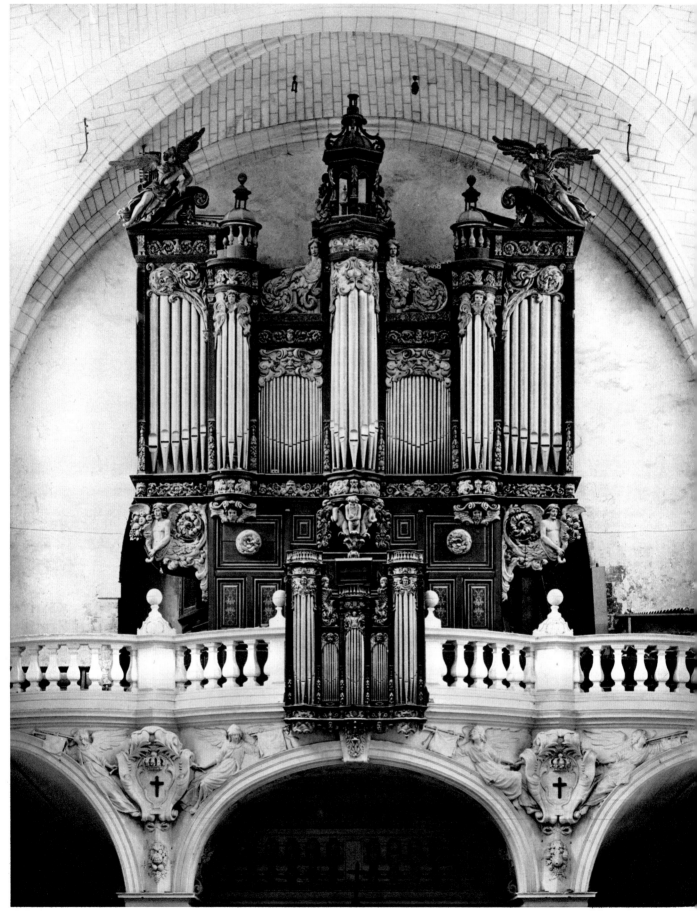

132   La Flèche (Sarthe), Chapelle du Prytanée Militaire, 1638

FRANCE

Paris, Saint-Étienne-du-Mont, 1636   133

FRANCE

134   Reims (Marne), Cathédrale Notre-Dame, 1620

FRANCE

Paris, Saint-Merry, *c.* 1651

FRANCE

136   Les Andelys (Eure), Saint-Sauveur du Petit-Andely, 1674

FRANCE

La Chaise-Dieu (Haute-Loire), Saint-Robert, *c*. 1675

137

FRANCE

138   Auch (Gers), Cathédrale Sainte-Marie, 1690

FRANCE

Marmoutier (Bas-Rhin), Église Abbatiale, 1709 139

140   Versailles (Seine-et-Oise), Château, Chapelle Saint-Louis, *c.* 1700

FRANCE

Saint-Omer (Pas-de-Calais), Notre-Dame, 1717   141

FRANCE

142   Aix-en-Provence (Bouches-du-Rhône), Cathédrale Saint-Sauveur, 1744

FRANCE

Uzès (Gard), Saint-Théodorit, *c.* 1685

143

FRANCE

144   Bayonne (Basses-Pyrénées), Cathédrale Sainte-Marie, *c.* 1750

FRANCE

Ébersmunster (Bas-Rhin), Église Abbatiale, 1728

FRANCE

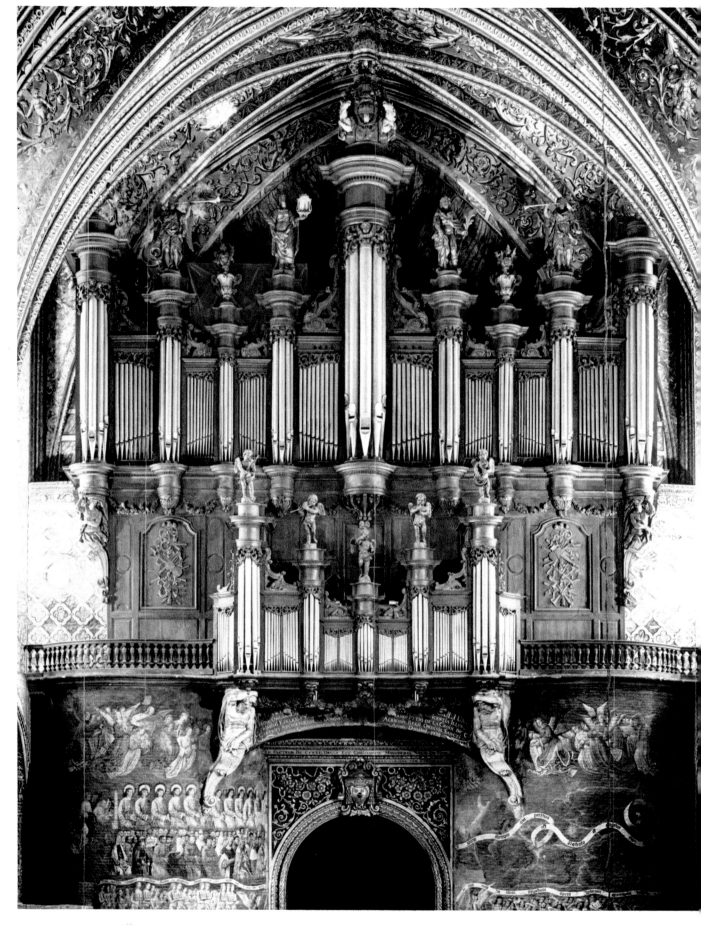

146 Albi (Tarn), Cathédrale Sainte-Cécile, 1736

FRANCE

Dijon (Côte-d'Or), Cathédrale Saint-Bénigne, 1743 147

148   Versailles, Château, orgue du Dauphin, *c.* 1745

FRANCE

Nancy (Meurthe-et-Moselle), Cathédrale Notre-Dame, 1756

FRANCE

150   Paris, Saint-Gervais-et-Saint-Protais, 1758

FRANCE

Saint-Maximin-la-Sainte-Baume (Var), Sainte-Marie-Madeleine, 1772   151

FRANCE

152   Bordeaux (Gironde), Saint-Seurin, 1773

FRANCE

Paris, Saint-Sulpice, 1779   153

FRANCE

154   Saint-Guilhem-le-Désert (Hérault), Église Abbatiale, 1789

FRANCE

Pithiviers (Loiret), Saint-Salomon-et-Saint-Grégoire, 1784   155

156   Orléans (Loiret), Cathédrale Sainte-Croix, 1703

FRANCE

Poitiers (Vienne), Cathédrale Saint-Pierre, 1789 157

FRANCE

158   Paris, Sainte-Marie-Madeleine (La Madeleine), 1844

FRANCE

Paris, Saint-Eustache, 1849   159

FRANCE

160   Paris, Sainte-Clotilde, *c.* 1857

FRANCE

Spain, Portugal

Salamanca (Leon, s), Catedral Vieja, Capilla de San Bartolomé, *c*. 1370

162   Zaragoza (Aragon, s), Catedral de La Seo, 1443

SPAIN, PORTUGAL

Zaragoza (Aragon, s), Catedral de La Seo, 1443

164   Calatayud (Aragon, S), San Pedro de los Francos, *c.* 1480

Toledo (s), Catedral, 1539   165

166   Salamanca (Leon, s), Catedral Nueva, Epistle organ, 1558

Barcelona (Catalonia, s), Catedral, 1539   167

SPAIN, PORTUGAL

168   Evora (Alto Alentejo, P), Catedral, 1562

SPAIN, PORTUGAL

Tarragona (Catalonia, s), Catedral, 1563

SPAIN, PORTUGAL

170   Tarragona (Catalonia, s), Catedral, 1563

SPAIN, PORTUGAL

Tarragona (Catalonia, s), Catedral, 1563   171

172   Huesca (Aragon, s), Catedral, 1761

SPAIN, PORTUGAL

Zaragoza (Aragon, s), Nuestra Señora del Pilar, 1527   173

SPAIN, PORTUGAL

174   Salamanca (Leon, s), Museo de la Catedral, *c.* 1550

SPAIN, PORTUGAL

Ciudad Rodrigo (Salamanca, s), Catedral, Gospel organ, *c.* 1650   175

176   Cádiz (Andalusia, s), Catedral Nueva, Gospel organ, *c.* 1680

SPAIN, PORTUGAL

Burgos (Old Castile, s), Catedral, Capilla del Condestable, *c.* 1530 177

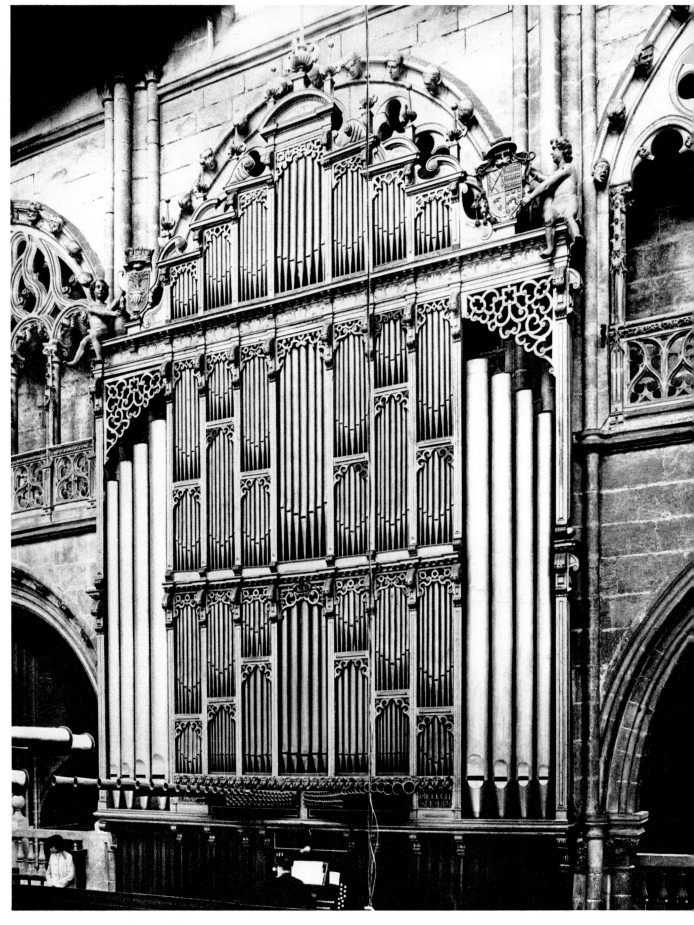

178   Burgos (Old Castile, s), Catedral, Epistle organ, 1645

Burgos (Old Castile, s), Catedral, Capilla de San Enrique, *c.* 1675

179

El Burgo de Osma (Soria, s), Catedral, Epistle organ, 1641

SPAIN, PORTUGAL

Ciudad Rodrigo (Salamanca, s), Catedral, Epistle organ, *c.* 1735   181

182   Orihuela (Alicante, s), Catedral, 1734

SPAIN, PORTUGAL

Tudela (Navarre, s), Catedral, *c.* 1680   183

184   Segovia (Old Castile, s), Catedral, Gospel organ 1772, Epistle organ 1702

SPAIN, PORTUGAL

Santiago de Compostela (La Coruña, s), Catedral, Gospel organ, 1705

185

186   Túy (Galicia, s), Catedral, 1712

SPAIN, PORTUGAL

Mondoñedo (Lugo, s), Catedral, Epistle organ, 1714   187

188   Braga (Minho, P), Catedral, 1737

Braga (Minho, P), Catedral, 1737   189

SPAIN, PORTUGAL

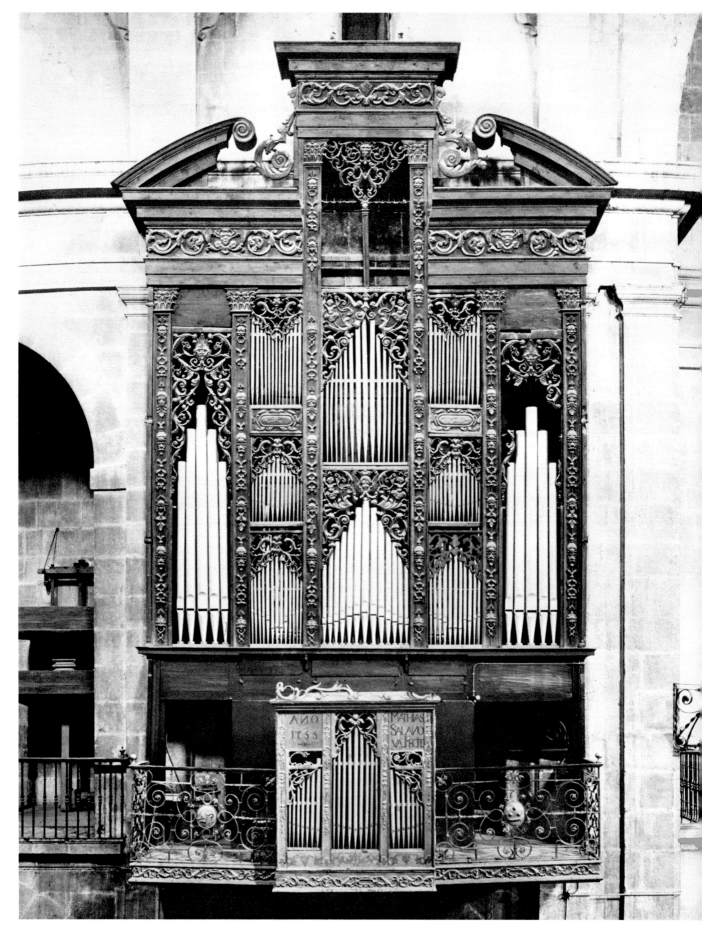

190   Alicante (s), San Nicolás de Bari, *c.* 1600

SPAIN, PORTUGAL

Toledo (s), Catedral, Epistle organ, 1758

SPAIN, PORTUGAL

192   Palencia (s), Catedral, 1716

SPAIN, PORTUGAL

Palencia (s), Catedral, 1716

SPAIN, PORTUGAL

194   Tarazona (Aragon, s), Catedral, 1766

Braga (P), Nossa Senhora da Lapa, *c.* 1750   195

196   Jaén (Andalusia, s), Catedral, Gospel organ, 1778

Málaga (Andalusia, s), Catedral, 1778   197

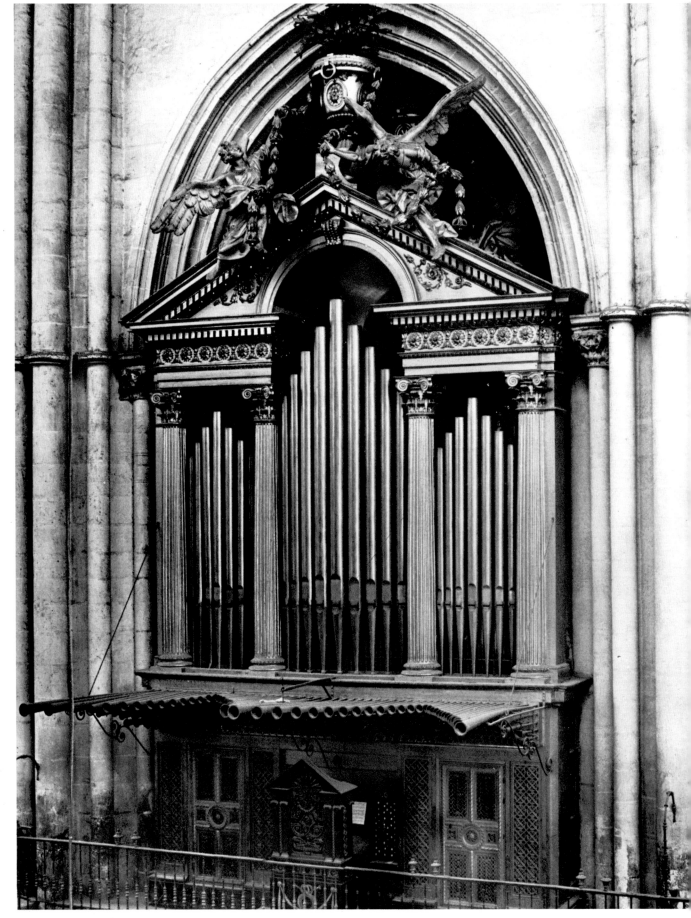

198   Toledo (s), Catedral, Gospel organ, 1796

SPAIN, PORTUGAL

Cádiz (Andalusia, s), Catedral Nueva, Epistle organ, 1862   199

200   Mafra (Lisboa, P), Convento, 1806

Mafra (Lisboa, P), Convento, 1806

SPAIN, PORTUGAL

202   Burgos (Old Castile, s), Catedral, Gospel organ, 1806

Coria (Caceres, s), Catedral, Gospel organ, 1806   203

SPAIN, PORTUGAL

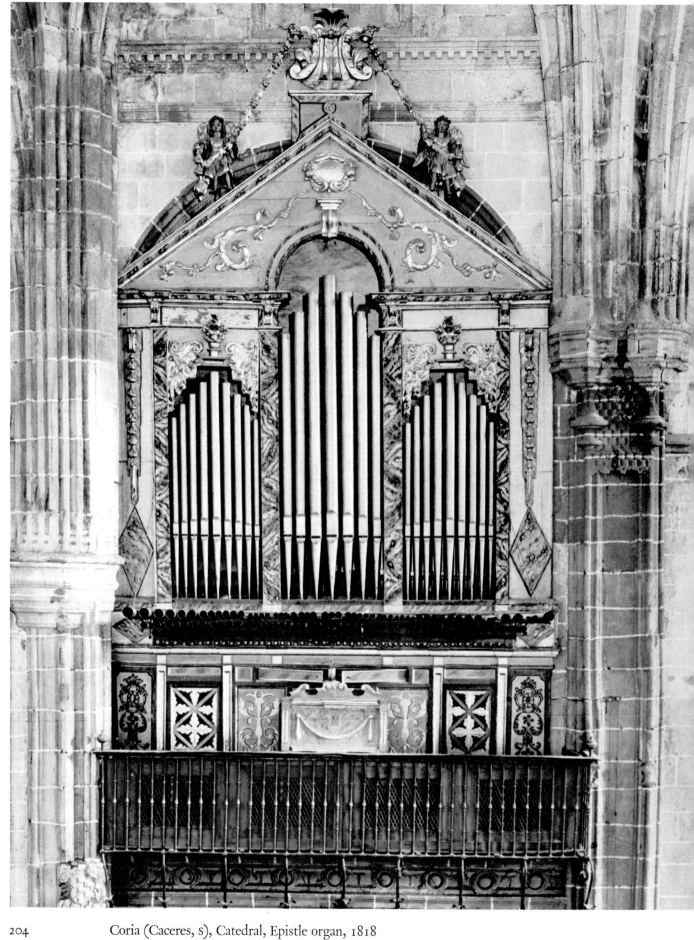

204   Coria (Caceres, s), Catedral, Epistle organ, 1818

SPAIN, PORTUGAL

Italy

Bologna, San Petronio, Epistle organ, *c.* 1480

ITALY

The inscription on the organ reads:

PRÆCINITE DOMINO
IN CONFESSIONE

206   Bologna, San Petronio, Epistle organ, *c.* 1480

ITALY

Perugia (Umbria), San Pietro, *c.* 1520

ITALY

208   Siena (Tuscany), Santa Maria della Scala, *c.* 1515

ITALY

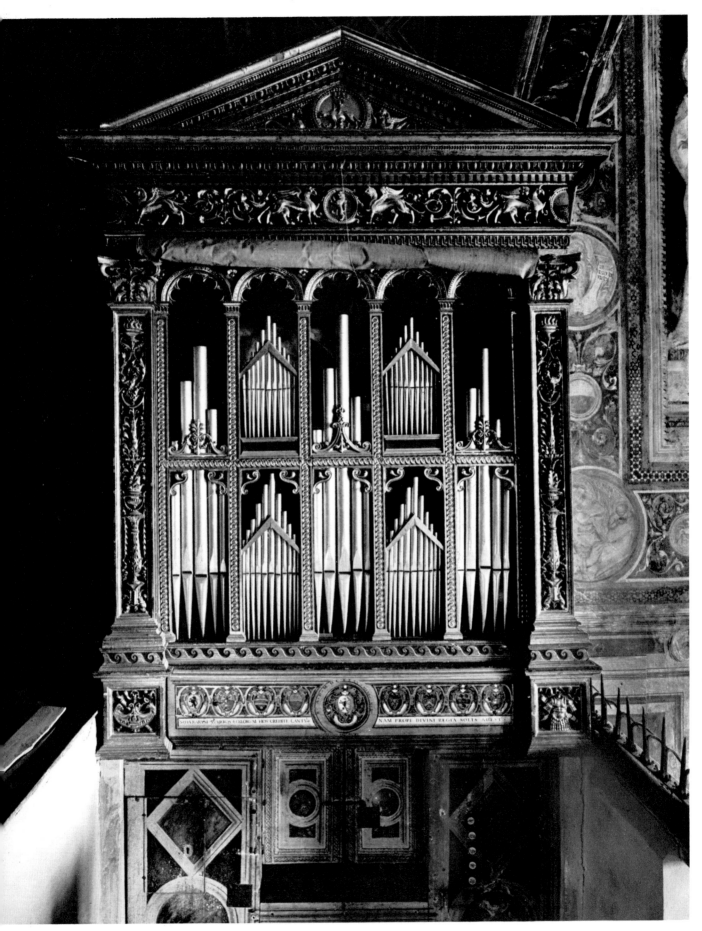

Siena (Tuscany), Palazzo Pubblico (Cappella), 1519   209

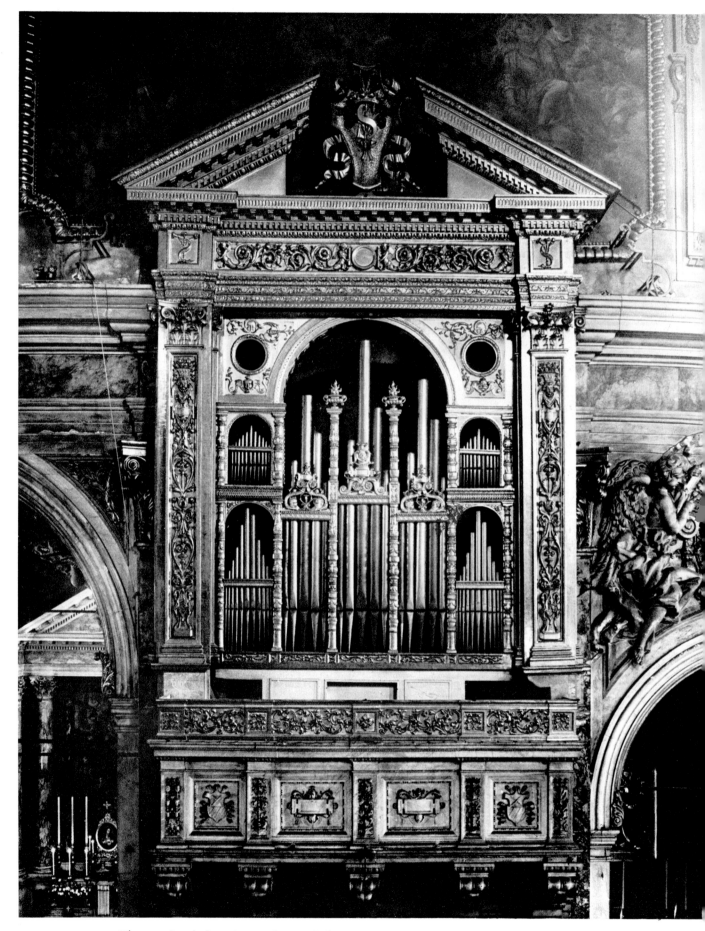

210   Firenze, Santissima Annunziata, Epistle organ, 1523

ITALY

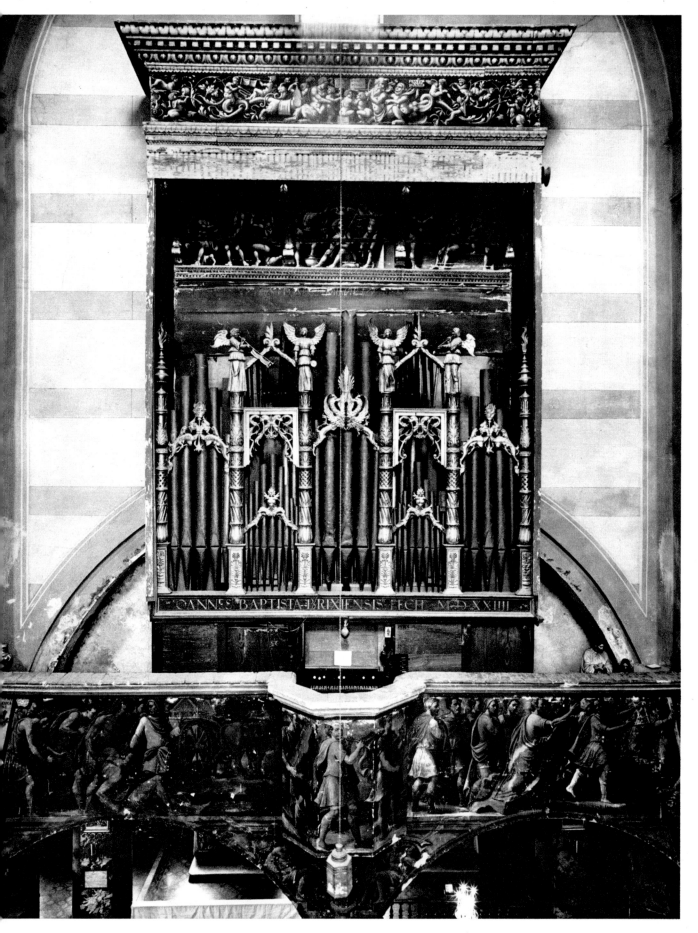

Modena, San Pietro, 1524

ITALY

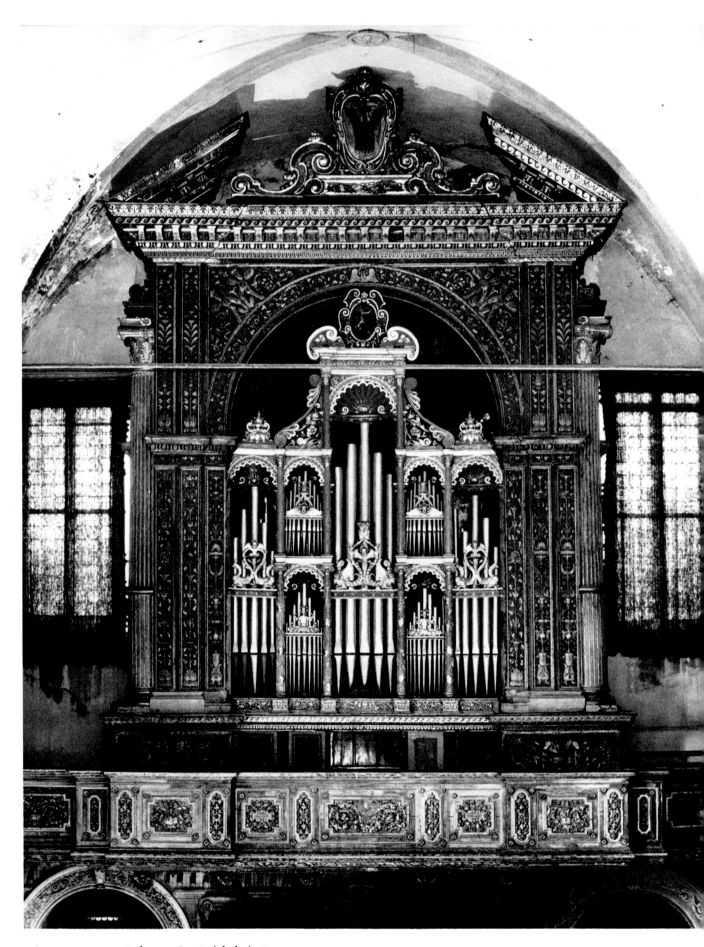

212   Bologna, San Michele in Bosco, 1524

ITALY

Brescia, Duomo Vecchio, 1536

ITALY

214   Genova, Cattedrale di San Lorenzo, 1552

ITALY

Bologna, San Martino, 1556   215

ITALY

216   Verona, Sant' Anastasia, restored 1560

ITALY

Milano, Santa Maria della Passione, Epistle organ, 1558   217

ITALY

218   Milano, Santa Maria della Passione, both organs

ITALY

220   Milano, Santa Maria della Passione, Gospel organ, 1613

ITALY

Orvieto (Umbria), Duomo, 1582   221

ITALY

REGNA TERRAE
CANT TE DEO

222   Bologna, San Petronio, Gospel organ, 1596 (1641)

ITALY

Bologna, San Petronio, Gospel organ, 1596 (1641) 223

ITALY

224   Roma, San Giovanni in Laterano, 1598

ITALY

Quinzano (Brescia), San Rocco, *c.* 1600

ITALY

226   Lucca (Tuscany), Duomo, Gospel organ, 1615

ITALY

Bologna, San Salvatore, 1620   227

ITALY

228   Pesaro, Oratorio del Santissimo Nome di Dio, *c.* 1625

ITALY

Roma, Santa Maria della Pace, *c.* 1650

229

ITALY

230   Roma, Santa Maria in Vallicella, *c.* 1660

ITALY

Genova, Santa Maria Assunta di Carignano, 1657   231

ITALY

232   Pistoia (Tuscany), Spirito Santo, 1669

ITALY

Bologna, Santi Gregorio e Siro, Gospel organ, 1673   233

ITALY

234 San Severino Marche (Macerata), San Severino al Monte, 1673

ITALY

Burgusio, Chiesa parrochiale, 1677 235

236   Napoli, San Gregorio Armeno, Gospel organ, *c.* 1650

ITALY

Napoli, San Gregorio Armeno, Epistle organ, *c.* 1650

237

ITALY

238   Ardesio, Santuario della Madonna delle Grazie, *c.* 1700

ITALY

Gandino (Bergamo), Santa Maria Assunta, *c.* 1700   239

ITALY

240   Grosotto, Santuario della Beata Vergine delle Grazie, 1706

ITALY

Rezzato (Brescia), Santa Maria in Valverde, 1716 241

242   Verona, San Tommaso Cantuariense, 1716

ITALY

L'Aquila, San Bernardino, *c.* 1725

243

ITALY

244   Bologna, San Domenico, Cappella del Rosario, *c.* 1720

ITALY

Udine, Duomo, Gospel organ, 1549?

ITALY

246   Venezia, San Giorgio Maggiore, *c.* 1730

ITALY

Fano (Pesaro/Urbino), San Paterniano, 1775 247

248   Venezia, San Raffaele Arcangelo, 1749

ITALY

British Isles

Old Radnor (Wales), St Stephen, *c.* 1530

Tewkesbury (Gloucestershire), Abbey Church, *c.* 1590

BRITISH ISLES

Cambridge, King's College Chapel, 1605

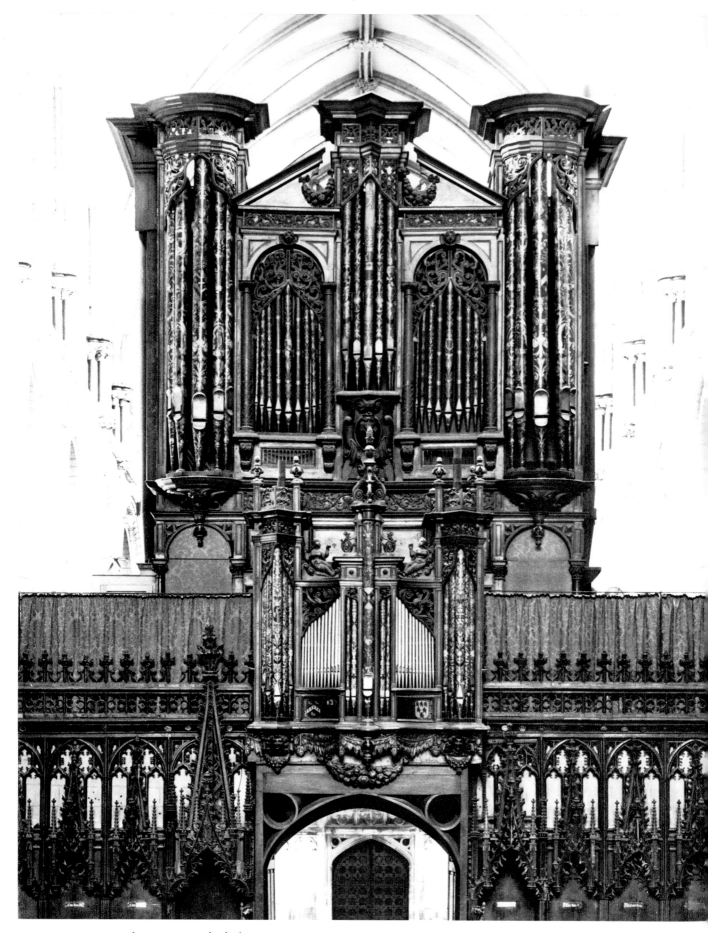

252   Gloucester, Cathedral, 1666

BRITISH ISLES

Exeter (Devonshire), Cathedral, 1665   253

254   Macclesfield (Cheshire), Adlington Hall, *c.* 1670

London, St Paul's Cathedral, 1695   255

256   London, the Tower, Chapel of St Peter-ad-Vincula, 1699

Twickenham (Middlesex), All Hallows, 1703   257

258   London, St Magnus the Martyr, 1712

London, St Vedast, 1731 259

King's Lynn (Norfolk), St Margaret, 1754

BRITISH ISLES

London, Greenwich, Chapel of the Royal Naval Hospital, 1789

BRITISH ISLES

Wymondham (Norfolk), Abbey Church, 1793

Lincoln, Cathedral, 1826   263

Lincoln, Cathedral, 1826

BRITISH ISLES

List of Plates

*The dates shown are, wherever possible, those of
the first year of building, not of completion.*

NETHERLANDS (NORTH)

1-3   Middelburg (Zeeland), Koorkerk, 1479

4   Alkmaar (Noord-Holland), Sint-Laurenskerk, choir organ, 1511

5   Amsterdam, Rijksmuseum, 1526

6   Jutphaas (Utrecht), Sint-Nicolaas, c. 1520

7   Monnikendam (Noord-Holland), Nederlandse Hervormde Kerk, c. 1530

8,9   Enkhuizen (Noord-Holland), Sint-Gommaruskerk, 1547

10   Abcoude (Utrecht), Sint-Cosmas-en-Damianus, 1556

11   Loppersum (Groningen), Nederlandse Hervormde Kerk, 1562

12   's-Hertogenbosch (Noord-Brabant), Kathedraal van Sint-Jan, 1618

13   Alkmaar (Noord-Holland), Sint-Laurenskerk, 1638

14   Zeerijp (Groningen), Nederlandse Hervormde Kerk, 1645

15   Dordrecht (Zuid-Holland), Onze-Lieve-Vrouwekerk, 1671

16   Medemblick (Noord-Holland), Nederlandse Hervormde Kerk, 1668.

17   Amsterdam, Waalse Kerk, 1680

18   Amsterdam, Westerkerk, 1686

19   Groningen, Martinikerk, 1542

20,21   Middelburg (Zeeland), Nieuwe Kerk, 1692

22   Groningen, A-Kerk, 1699

23   Culemborg (Gelderland), Sint-Barbarakerk, 1719

24   Zwolle (Overijssel), Sint-Michaëlskerk, 1721

25   's-Gravenhage (Zuid-Holland), Oud-Katholieke Kerk, 1724

26   Amsterdam, Oude Kerk, 1726

27   Leens (Groningen), Nederlandse Hervormde Kerk, c. 1735

28   Gouda (Zuid-Holland), Sint-Janskerk, 1732

29   Haarlem (Noord-Holland), Sint-Bavokerk, 1735

30   Teeffelen (Noord-Braband), Sint-Benedictus, c. 1750

31   Nijkerk (Gelderland), Nederlandse Hervormde Kerk, 1756

32   's-Gravenhage, Morgensternkerk, c. 1740

33   Helmond (Noord-Brabant), Sint-Lambertus, 1771

34   Schiedam (Zuid-Holland), Stedelijk Museum, 1773

35   Amsterdam, Sint-Franciscus-van-Assisië, c. 1775

36   Leiderdorp (Zuid-Holland), Nederlandse Hervormde Kerk, 1781

37   Bolsward (Friesland), Martinikerk, c. 1775

38   Amsterdam, Stichting Amstelhof, c. 1825

39   Elburg (Gelderland), Nederlandse Hervormde Kerk, 1825

40   Boxtel (Noord-Brabant), Sint-Petrus, 1842

41   Schijndel (Noord-Brabant), Sint-Serviatus, 1839

42   Naarden (Noord-Holland), Sint-Vituskerk, 1862

NETHERLANDS (SOUTH)

43 Tienen (Brabant), Sint-Germanus, *c.* 1516
44 Quenast (Brabant), Saint-Martin, 1540
45 Liège, Saint-Denis, 1589
46 Liège, Saint-Jacques, 1600
47 Lier (Antwerp), Sint-Gummarus, 1628
48 Watervliet (Oost-Vlaanderen), Onze-Lieve-Vrouw-Hemelvaart, 1643
49 Lissewege (West-Vlaanderen), Onze-Lieve-Vrouw, 1653
50 Gent (Oost-Vlaanderen), Sint-Baafskathedraal, 1653
51 Antwerp, Sint-Paulus, 1648
52 Mechlin (Antwerp), Onze-Lieve-Vrouw-over-de-Dijle, 1665
53 Saint-Hubert (Luxembourg), Basilique Saint-Hubert, 1685
54 Stalhille (West-Vlaanderen), Sint-Jan-Baptist, 1715
55 Bruges (West-Vlaanderen), Sint-Salvatorkathedraal, 1717
56 Antwerp, Sint-Carolus, *c.* 1720
57 Antwerp, Sint-Jacob, 1727
58 Tournai (Hainaut), Saint-Jacques, 1753
59 Tongeren (Limburg), Onze-Lieve-Vrouw, *c.* 1750
60 Poperinge (West-Vlaanderen), Onze-Lieve-Vrouw, *c.* 1760
61 Mechlin (Antwerp). Sint-Jan, 1759
62 Haringe (West-Vlaanderen), Sint-Martinus, 1778
63 Belsele (Oost-Vlaanderen), Sint-Andries-en-Ghislanus, 1784
64 Averbode (Brabant), Abdij, 1853

AUSTRIA, GERMANY, SWITZERLAND

65 Sion (Valais, SW), Notre-Dame-de-Valère, *c.* 1400
66 Kiedrich (Hessen, G), Sankt Valentin, *c.* 1495
67 Lübeck (Schleswig-Holstein, G), Sankt Jakobi, small organ, *c.* 1500
68 Innsbruck (Tirol, A), Silberne Kapelle, *c.* 1550
69 Augsburg (Bayern, G), Sankt Anna, Fuggerkapelle, *c.* 1512 (reconstructed)
70 Konstanz (Baden-Württemberg, G), Münster, 1516
71 Nördlingen (Bayern, G), Sankt Georg, 1466
72 Klosterneuburg (Niederösterreich, A), Stiftskirche, 1642
73 Stade (Niedersachsen, G), Sankt Cosmae-et-Damiani, 1669
74 Corvey (Nordrhein-Westfalen, G), Klosterkirche, 1681
75 Neuenfelde (Hamburg, G), Sankt Pankratii, 1688
76 Landshut (Bayern, G), Sankt Martin, 1700
77 Sankt Urban (Luzern, SW), Klosterkirche, 1716
78 Innsbruck (Tirol, A), Sankt Jakob, 1725
79 Ochsenhausen (Baden-Württemberg, G), Klosterkirche, 1729
80 Borgentreich (Nordrhein-Westfalen G), Sankt Johannes Baptist, 1730
81 Sankt Peter (Baden-Württemberg, G), Klosterkirche, 1732
82 Melk (Niederösterreich, A), Stiftskirche, 1732
83–85 Weingarten (Baden-Württemberg, G), Klosterkirche, 1737
86 Rottenbuch (Bayern, G), Mariä-Geburt-Kirche, 1747
87 Marienfeld (Nordrhein-Westfalen, G), Klosterkirche, 1751
88 Einsiedeln (Schwyz, SW), Klosterkirche, 1751
89 Esslingen (Baden-Württemberg, G), Sankt Dionysius, 1706
90 Irsee (Bayern, G), Klosterkirche, 1754

91 Die Wies (Bayern, G), Wallfahrtskirche, c. 1756
92 Ottobeuren (Bayern, G), Klosterkirche, Holy Ghost organ, 1764
93 Ottobeuren, Trinity organ
94 Ottobeuren, Holy Ghost organ
95 Roggenburg (Bayern, G), Stiftskirche, 1752
96 Arlesheim (Baselland, sw), Dom, 1759
97 Fischingen (Thurgau, sw), Klosterkirche, 1763
98 Ettal (Bayern, G), Klosterkirche, 1763
99 Bregenz (Vorarlberg, A), Sankt Gallus, 1771
100 Hilzingen (Baden-Württemberg, G), Sankt Peter-und-Paul, c. 1770
101 Salem (Baden-Württemberg, G), Klosterkirche, 1770
102 Steingaden (Bayern, G), Klosterkirche, 1743
103 Amorbach (Bayern, G), Abteikirche, 1774
104 Einsiedeln (Schwyz, sw), Klosterkirche, Gospel organ, 1749
105 Einsiedeln, Epistle organ
106 Sankt Florian (Oberösterreich, A), Stiftskirche, 1770
107 Schwyz (sw), Sankt Martin, 1778
108 Neresheim (Baden-Württemberg, G), Klosterkirche, 1797
109 Hof-an-der-Saale (Bayern, G), Sankt Michaelis, 1834
110 Giengen-an-der-Brenz (Baden-Württemberg, G), Sankt Marien, 1905

DENMARK
111 Sorø (Sjaelland) Klosterkirke, c. 1550
112 Roskilde (Sjaelland), Domkirke, 1555
113 Hillerød (Sjaelland), Frederiksborg Slotskirke, Compenius organ, 1610
114 Hillerød, Frederiksborg Slotskirke, Lorenz organ, 1614 (reconstructed)
115 Haderslev (Jylland), Domkirke, 1652
116 København, Vor Frelsers Kirke, 1698
117 København, Holmens Kirke, 1740
118 Odense (Fyn), Domkirke, 1752

FRANCE
119 Strasbourg (Bas-Rhin), Cathédrale Notre-Dame, 1489
120 Perpignan (Pyrénées-Orientales), Cathédrale Saint-Jean, c. 1500
121 Amiens (Somme), Cathédrale Notre-Dame, 1549
122 Tours (Indre-et-Loire), Cathédrale Saint-Gatien, 1562
123 La Ferté-Bernard (Sarthe), Notre-Dame-des-Marais, 1536
124 Saint-Bertrand-de-Comminges (Haute-Garonne), Cathédrale Notre-Dame, 1536
125 Caudebec-en-Caux (Seine-Maritime), Notre-Dame, 1542
126 Chartres (Eure-et-Loire), Cathédrale Notre-Dame, 1542
127 Les Andelys (Eure), Notre-Dame du Grand-Andely, 1573
128 Rodez (Aveyron), Cathédrale Notre-Dame, 1628
129 Toulouse (Haute-Garonne), Cathédrale Saint-Étienne, c. 1611
130 Embrun (Hautes-Alpes), Notre-Dame, 1463
131 Rouen (Seine-Maritime), Saint-Ouen, 1630
132 La Flèche (Sarthe), Chapelle du Prytanée Militaire, 1638
133 Paris, Saint-Étienne-du-Mont, 1636
134 Reims (Marne), Cathédrale Notre-Dame, 1620
135 Paris, Saint-Merry, c. 1651

136   Les Andelys, Saint-Sauveur du Petit-Andely, 1674

137   La Chaise-Dieu (Haute-Loire), Saint-Robert, c. 1675

138   Auch (Gers), Cathédrale Sainte-Marie, 1690

139   Marmoutier (Bas-Rhin), Église Abbatiale, 1709

140   Versailles (Seine-et-Oise), Château, Chapelle Saint-Louis, c. 1700

141   Saint-Omer (Pas-de-Calais), Notre-Dame, 1717

142   Aix-en-Provence (Bouches-du-Rhône), Cathédrale Saint-Sauveur, 1744

143   Uzès (Gard), Saint-Théodorit, c. 1685

144   Bayonne (Basses-Pyrénées), Cathédrale Sainte-Marie, c. 1750

145   Ébersmunster (Bas-Rhin), Église Abbatiale, 1728

146   Albi (Tarn), Cathédrale Sainte-Cécile, 1736

147   Dijon (Côte-d'Or), Cathédrale Saint-Bénigne, 1743

148   Versailles, Château, orgue du Dauphin, c. 1745

149   Nancy (Meurthe-et-Moselle), Cathédrale Notre-Dame, 1756

150   Paris, Saint-Gervais-et-Saint-Protais, 1758

151   Saint-Maximin-la-Sainte-Baume (Var), Sainte-Marie-Madeleine, 1772

152   Bordeaux (Gironde), Saint-Seurin, 1773

153   Paris, Saint-Sulpice, 1779

154   Saint-Guilhem-le-Désert (Hérault), Église Abbatiale, 1789

155   Pithiviers (Loiret), Saint-Salomon-et-Saint-Grégoire, 1784

156   Orléans (Loiret), Cathédrale Sainte-Croix, 1703

157   Poitiers (Vienne), Cathédrale Saint-Pierre, 1789

158   Paris, Sainte-Marie-Madeleine (La Madeleine), 1844

159   Paris, Saint-Eustache, 1849

160   Paris, Sainte-Clotilde, c. 1857

SPAIN, PORTUGAL

161   Salamanca (Leon, s), Catedral Vieja, Capilla de San Bartolomé, c. 1370

162, 163   Zaragoza (Aragon, s), Catedral de La Seo, 1443

164   Calatayud (Aragon, s), San Pedro de los Francos, c. 1480

165   Toledo (s), Catedral, 1539

166   Salamanca (Leon, s), Catedral Nueva, Epistle organ, 1558

167   Barcelona (Catalonia, s), Catedral, 1539

168   Evora (Alto Alentejo, p), Catedral, 1562

169–171   Tarragona (Catalonia, s), Catedral, 1563

172   Huesca (Aragon, s), Catedral, 1761

173   Zaragoza (Aragon, s), Nuestra Señora del Pilar, 1527

174   Salamanca (Leon, s), Museo de la Catedral, c. 1550

175   Ciudad Rodrigo (Salamanca, s), Catedral, Gospel organ, c. 1650

176   Cádiz (Andalusia, s), Catedral Nueva, Gospel organ, c. 1680

177   Burgos (Old Castile, s), Catedral, Capilla del Condestable, c. 1530

178   Burgos (Old Castile, s), Catedral, Epistle organ, 1645

179   Burgos (Old Castile, s), Catedral, Capilla de San Enrique, c. 1675

180   El Burgo de Osma (Soria, s), Catedral, Epistle organ, 1641

181   Ciudad Rodrigo (Salamanca, s), Catedral, Epistle organ, c. 1735

182   Orihuela (Alicante, s), Catedral, 1734

183   Tudela (Navarre, s), Catedral, c. 1680

184   Segovia (Old Castile, s), Catedral, Gospel organ 1772, Epistle organ 1702

185   Santiago de Compostela (La Coruña, s), Catedral, Gospel organ, 1705

186   Túy (Galicia, s), Catedral, 1712

187   Mondoñedo (Lugo, s), Catedral, Epistle organ, 1714

188, 189   Braga (Minho, p), Catedral, 1737

190   Alicante (s), San Nicolás de Bari, *c.* 1600

191   Toledo (s), Catedral, Epistle organ, 1758

192, 193   Palencia (s), Catedral, 1716

194   Tarazona (Aragon, s), Catedral, 1766

195   Braga (p), Nossa Senhora da Lapa, *c.* 1750

196   Jaén (Andalusia, s), Catedral, Gospel organ, 1778

197   Málaga (Andalusia, s), Catedral, 1778

198   Toledo (s), Catedral, Gospel organ, 1796

199   Cádiz (Andalusia, s), Catedral Nueva, Epistle organ, 1862

200, 201   Mafra (Lisboa, p), Convento, 1806

202   Burgos (Old Castile, s), Catedral, Gospel organ, 1806

203   Coria (Caceres, s), Catedral, Gospel organ, 1806

204   Coria (Caceres, s), Catedral, Epistle organ, 1818

ITALY

205, 206   Bologna, San Petronio, Epistle organ, *c.* 1480

207   Perugia (Umbria), San Pietro, *c.* 1520

208   Siena (Tuscany), Santa Maria della Scala, *c.* 1515

209   Siena (Tuscany), Palazzo Pubblico (Cappella), 1519

210   Firenze, Santissima Annunziata, Epistle organ, 1523

211   Modena, San Pietro, 1524

212   Bologna, San Michele in Bosco, 1524

213   Brescia, Duomo Vecchio, 1536

214   Genova, Cattedrale di San Lorenzo, 1552

215   Bologna, San Martino, 1556

216   Verona, Sant'Anastasia, restored 1560

217   Milano, Santa Maria della Passione, Epistle organ, 1558

218, 219   Milano, Santa Maria della Passione, both organs

220   Milano, Santa Maria della Passione, Gospel organ, 1613

221   Orvieto (Umbria), Duomo, 1582

222, 223   Bologna, San Petronio, Gospel organ, 1596 (1641)

224   Roma, San Giovanni in Laterano, 1598

225   Quinzano (Brescia), San Rocco, *c.* 1600

226   Lucca (Tuscany), Duomo, Gospel organ, 1615

227   Bologna, San Salvatore, 1620

228   Pesaro, Oratorio del Santissimo Nome di Dio, *c.* 1625

229   Roma, Santa Maria della Pace, *c.* 1650

230   Roma, Santa Maria in Vallicella, *c.* 1660

231   Genova, Santa Maria Assunta di Carignano, 1657

232   Pistoia (Tuscany), Spirito Santo, 1669

233   Bologna, Santi Gregorio e Siro, Gospel organ, 1673

234   San Severino Marche (Macerata), San Severino al Monte, 1673

235   Burgusio, Chiesa parrochiale, 1677

236   Napoli, San Gregorio Armeno, Gospel organ, *c.* 1650

237   Napoli, San Gregorio Armeno, Epistle organ, *c.* 1650

238   Ardesio, Santuario della Madonna delle Grazie, *c.* 1700

239 Gandino (Bergamo), Santa Maria Assunta, *c.* 1700
240 Grosotto, Santuario della Beata Vergine delle Grazie, 1706
241 Rezzato (Brescia), Santa Maria in Valverde, 1716
242 Verona, San Tommaso Cantuariense, 1716
243 L'Aquila, San Bernardino, *c.* 1725
244 Bologna, San Domenico, Cappella del Rosario, *c.* 1720
245 Udine, Duomo, Gospel organ, 1549?
246 Venezia, San Giorgio Maggiore, *c.* 1730
247 Fano (Pesaro/Urbino), San Paterniano, 1775
248 Venezia, San Raffaele Arcangelo, 1749

BRITISH ISLES
249 Old Radnor (Wales), St Stephen, *c.* 1530
250 Tewkesbury (Gloucestershire), Abbey Church, *c.* 1590
251 Cambridge, King's College Chapel, 1605
252 Gloucester, Cathedral, 1666
253 Exeter (Devonshire), Cathedral, 1665
254 Macclesfield (Cheshire), Adlington Hall, *c.* 1670
255 London, St Paul's Cathedral, 1695
256 London, the Tower, Chapel of St Peter-ad-Vincula, 1699
257 Twickenham (Middlesex), All Hallows, 1703
258 London, St Magnus the Martyr, 1712
259 London, St Vedast, 1731
260 King's Lynn (Norfolk), St Margaret, 1754
261 London, Greenwich, Chapel of the Royal Naval Hospital, 1789
262 Wymondham (Norfolk), Abbey Church, 1793
263, 264 Lincoln, Cathedral, 1826

Lists of the various artists and craftsmen mentioned in this book

Organ Builders

AGUIRRE, Domingo de, d. 1725. (192, 193)
AICHGASSER, Johann Georg, fl. 1763. (97)
ALLEN, Charles, fl. c. 1840–50. (264)
ALLEN, William, fl. c. 1790–1825. (263, 264)
ALLGEYER, Georg, fl. 1706. (89)
AMIGAZZI, Gaetano, fl. 1749. (248)
ANTEGNATI, Costanzo, fl. c. 1600–8. (225)
ANTEGNATI, Gian Giacomo, fl. 1536–58. (213, 217–20)
ARGUETA, Juan de, fl. 1636. (178)
ARNAUT, Henri, fl. 1440. (65)
BACKER, Pieter E., fl. 1668–71. (16)
BENVENUTI, Domenico, fl. 1579. (221)
BETOZALA, Juan Manuel, fl. 1806. (202)
BIS, Louis, fl. 1650–3. (50)
BIASI, Luca, fl. 1597–99. (224)
BONATTI, Giuseppe, 1668–1752. (241, 242)
BOSSART, Joseph, fl. 1716–21. (77)
BOSSART, Viktor Ferdinand, fl. 1751–4. (88)
BOTZ, Peter Karstensen, fl. 1652. (115)
BOTZEN, Johann and Peter Petersen, fl. 1698–1700. (116)
BOUTHILLIER, Franz Joseph, fl. 1778–80. (107)
BREMSER, Jan, c. 1610–69. (52)
BYFIELD, John I, d. 1757. (259)
CALLIDO, Gaetano, 1727–1813. (247)
CARLIER, Crespin, fl. c. 1600. (131)
CATARINOZZI, Giuseppe, fl. 1673. (234)
CAVAILLÉ, Jean-Pierre, d. 1809. (154)
CAVAILLÉ-COLL, Aristide, 1811–99. (153, 158, 160)
CHRISMANN, Franz Xaver, fl. 1770–4. (106)
CIPRI, Giovanni fl. 1555–60. (215, 216)
CLAES, Allaert, fl. 1555. (4)
CLIQUOT, François-Henri, 1732–90. (153, 157)
COCQUEREL, Antoine-Josseline and Gilbert, fl. 1542–3. (125)
COLOMBI, Vincenzo, fl. 1549–50. (245)
COLONNA, Vincenzo, fl. 1620–1. (227)
COVELEN, Jan van (Johann von Koblenz), fl. 1511–20. (4, 6, 7)
DABENET, Nicolas, fl. 1573. (127)
DAL CORNO, Antonio, fl. 1620–1. (227)
DALLAM, Thomas, c. 1575–c. 1630. (251)
DAVIS, James, d. 1827. (262)
DE LA ORDEN, Julián, fl. 1778. (197)
DE LA VIÑA, Manuel, fl. c. 1705–22. (185, 187)
DESFONTAINES, Jean-Jacques and Thomas, fl. 1715–17. (141)
DESTRE, Pierre, fl. 1650–3. (50)
DEVENTER, Matthijs van, fl. 1756. (31)
DUCROQUET, *Messrs*, fl. c. 1850. (159)

DUPONT, Joseph and Nicolas, fl. 1756–7. (149)
DUYSCHOT, Jan, fl. 1686–92. (18, 20, 21)
ECHEVARRÍA, Pedro Liborna, fl. 1758. (191)
EMEDENSIS, Johannes, fl. 1526. (5)
EYNDE, Jacobus van, fl. 1696–1729. (54, 55)
FABER, Theodor, fl. 1645–53. (14)
FACCHETTI, Giovanni Battista, fl. 1519–52. (211, 212, 214)
FILLCUL, Robert, fl. 1542–51. (126)
FISCHER, Johann Georg, fl. 1732. (81)
FLORENZANO, Domingo, fl. 1806. (203)
FORCEVILLE (Forcivil), Jean-Baptiste, c. 1660–1739. (56, 57)
FREIWISS, Balthasar, fl. 1747–54. (86, 90)
FREUNDT, Johann Georg, fl. 1636–42. (72)
GABLER, Joseph, 1700–71. (79, 83/85, 99)
GARRELS, Rudolf, fl. 1724. (25)
GERRITSZ, Peter, fl. 1477–1535. (1/3)
GIACOMO, Lorenzo di, fl. 1470–5. (205, 206)
GREEN, Samuel, 1740–96. (261)
HAEGHEN, Nicolaes van, fl. 1645–82. (15, 51)
HAGEBEER, Germer van, fl. 1640. (13)
HARRIS, John, d. 1743. (259)
HARRIS, Renatus, 1652–1724. (251, 257)
HARRIS, Thomas, d. c. 1685. (252)
HEIDENREICH, brothers, fl. 1834. (109)
HERMANS, Willem, fl. 1650–73. (231, 232)
HESS, H. H., fl. 1773. (34)
HINSCH, Albert Anthoni, fl. 1735–84. (27, 37)
HOERTERICH, Johann Georg, fl. 1763. (98)
HOLZHAY, Johann Nepomuk, fl. 1785–97. (108)
HUESS, Berendt, fl. 1669–73. (73)
HUMPEL, Johann Caspar, fl. 1725. (78)
INGOUT, Robert, fl. 1674. (136)
ISNARD, Jean-Baptiste, 1726–1800. (151, 155)
ISNARD, Jean-Esprit, fl. 1744–81. (142, 151)
JAEGER, Andreas, fl. 1756–9. (91)
JORDAN, Abraham I and II, fl. 1700–46. (258)
JOYEUSE, Jean de, c. 1635–98, (138)
KASTENS, Lambert Daniel, fl. 1722–6. (117)
KLOTZ, Benedikt, fl. 1544–6. (71)
KREBS, Friedrich, fl. 1489–91. (119)
LANGLEZ, Nicolas, fl. 1680. (17)
LE DOU, Baudewyn, fl. 1643–5. (48, 49)
LEFEBVRE, Antoine, fl. 1611. (129)
LE PICARD, Jean-Baptiste, 1706–c. 1756. (59)
LEVASSEUR, Ambroise, fl. 1638–40. (132)
LINK, brothers, fl. 1905. (110)
LOOSEMORE, John, 1613–81. (253)
LORENZ, Johann, fl. 1627–8. (111, 114)

LORENZO, Domenico di, fl. 1523. (210)
LORET, Hippolyte, 1810–79. (64)
MAAS, Nikolaus, fl. 1604–8. (114)
MALAMINI, Baldassare, fl. 1596. (222)
MARE, Andreas de, fl. 1542. (19)
MAYO, Quintin, fl. 1641. (180)
MICOT, Jean-Baptiste, fl. 1771–6. (152)
MITTELREYTER, Johann, fl. 1781. (36)
MOELLER, Johann Patroclus, fl. 1730–51. (80, 87)
MOREAU, Jacob François, c. 1680–1756. (28)
MOUCHEREL, Christophe, 1686–1761(?). (146)
MUELLER, Christiaan, fl. 1735–8. (29)
NADAR DA PONCE, Antonio, fl. 1818. (204)
NIEHOFF, Hendrik, d. 1561. (8, 9, 10)
NIEHOFF, Nicolaes, c. 1525–c. 1604. (45)
PEASE, Lancelot, fl. 1662–81. (251)
PESCHEUR, Pierre, fl. 1620–31. (133)
PETEGHEM, Lambertus Benoît van, 1742–1807. (62, 63)
PETEGHEM, Pieter van I, 1708–87. (61, 62, 63)
PICARD, Antoine, fl. 1685. (53)
PIFFARO, Giovanni di Antonio, fl. 1516–23. (208, 209)
POCK, Herman Rafaelis Rodensteen, fl. 1555. (112)
PRATI, Carlo, fl. 1677–8. (235)
QUELLHORST, G. H., fl. 1825. (39)
RAINA, Giovanni Battista, fl. c. 1705. (240)
RAINA, Giuseppe, fl. 1730. (240)
RAVANI, Andrea and Cosimo, fl. 1615. (226)
RIEPP, Karl Joseph, 1710–75. (92–94, 101, 147)
ROBUSTELLY, Guillaume, fl. 1771. (33)
RYCKERE, Jean and Pierre-Joseph de, fl. 1753–82. (58)
SCHMAHL, Georg Friedrich, fl. 1752–61. (95)
SCHNEIDER, Andreas, fl. 1681. (74)
SCHNITGER, Arp, 1648–1719. (19, 22, 24, 73, 75)
SCHNITGER, Franz Caspar, 1693–1729. (13, 24)
SCHNITGER, Johann Jürgen, 1690–c. 1734. (24)
SILBERMANN, Andreas, 1678–1734, (119, 139, 145)
SILBERMANN, Johann Andreas, 1712–83. (96)
SMITH, Bernard, d. 1708. (254, 255, 256)
SMITS, François Corneille, 1800–post 1862, (40. 41)
SNETZLER, Johann, 1710–85. (260)
SOMER, Nicolas, fl. 1747. (148)
SONNHOLZ, Gottfried, fl. 1732. (82)
STELLWAGEN, Friedrich, fl. 1637. (67)
STUMM, Johann Heinrich and Johann Philipp, fl. 1774–82. (103)
THOMASZ, Dirck, fl. c. 1650. (13)
TRAERI, Carlo, fl. 1673. (233)
TRAERI, Giovanni Francesco, fl. 1724. (212)
VATER, Christian, fl. 1726. (26)
VERDALONGA, José, fl. 1796. (198)
VERHOFSTAD, M., fl. 1719. (23)
VERNHOLLES, Antoine, fl. 1628. (128)
VERRYDT, Jan, fl. 1535. (44)
WITTE, C. G. F., 1802–post 1864. (42)
WORM, Amdi, b. 1722. (118)
XIMENEZ, Fernandez, fl. 1530. (177)

Architects

ALDEHUELA, José Martín de, fl. 1778. (197)
AMIGÓ, Jaime, fl. c. 1550–86. (169–171)

ANDRADE, Domingo Antonio de, fl. 1700. (185)
BALTARD, Victor, 1805–63. (159)
CAMPEN, Jacob van, 1595–1657. (13)
CHALGRIN, Jean-François-Thérèse, 1739–1811. (153)
COTTE, Robert de, 1656–1735. (140)
COVARRUBIAS, Alonso de, c. 1448–1564. (165)
GAU, Franz Christian, 1790–1853. (160)
HAAM, Ignacio, fl. c. 1795. (198)
HUVÉ, Jean-Jacques-Marie, 1783–1852. (158)
JENNESSON, Jean-Nicolas, 1686–1755. (149)
LARA Y CHURRIGUERA, Manuel de, fl. c. 1721–39. (181)
MANSARD, Jules-Hardouin, 1645–1708. (140)
PERUZZI, Baldassare, 1481–1536. (208)
SCALZA, Ippolito, 1532–1617. (221)
SUTTON, Sir John, 1820–73. (66)
VERBURG, A., fl. 1730. (19)
WENZINGER, Johann Christian, 1710–97. (81)
WERFF, Hendrik de, fl. 1735–8. (29)
WILLSON, Edward James, 1787–1854. (263, 264)
WREN, Sir Christopher, 1632–1723. (255)
ZIMMERMANN, Dominikus, 1685–1766. (91)

Painters

AMALTEO, Pomponio, 1510–88. (245)
ANSOLDO DA VOLTRI, Andrea, 1584–1638. (214)
ASSELIJN, Jan, 1610–52 (or 1660). (6)
BREU, Jörg I, 1480–1537. (69)
BROZZI, Paolo, fl. c. 1650–60. (231)
BURGKMAIR, Hans, 1473–1531 (or 1553 or 1559). (69)
CAMPION, John, fl. c. 1660. (252)
CARRÉ, Hendrik II, 1696–1775. (28)
CRISPI, Daniele, fl. 1613. (217–220)
EVERDINGEN, Caspar van, fl. 1643. (13)
FURTADO, Manuel, fl. 1738. (188/189)
GEBRANDSZ, Hendrik, fl. 1643. (13)
GHINO D'ANTONIO, fl. c. 1525–45. (208)
GUTRECHT, Matheus II, fl. 1516–20. (70)
HERLIN, Jesse II, 1500–75. (71)
LAIRESSE, Gérard de, 1641–1711. (18)
LIMBORCH, Hendrik van, 1681–1759. (29)
MAGGENBERG, Peter, fl. 1434–7. (65)
MARTIN, August, 1837–1901. (66)
METZGER, Johann Simon, d. 1629. (71)
MONTEJO, Francisco de, fl. c. 1550. (166)
PABLO, Pedro, fl. 1563. (169–171)
PIOLA, Domenico I, 1627–1703. (231)
POMPEO DI ANSELMO, c. 1489–1517. (207)
QUELLIN (Quellinus), Erasmus II, 1607–78. (51)
ROMANINO, Girolamo, c. 1484–c. 1562. (213)
SANRAEDAM, Pieter Jansz, 1597–1665. (13)
SEFARÍ, Pedro, fl. 1563. (169–171)
SPANJAERT, Adrijaan, fl. 1668–71. (16)
TARZA, Antonio, fl. c. 1550. (166)
TERMONIA, Martin Benoît, fl. 1724–59. (59)
TERRASCHI, Giovanni and Giulio, fl. 1519. (211)
THIESSÉ, Pierre-Claude, fl. 1758–9. (150)
TIDEMANN, Philip, 1657–1705. (20, 21)
TURCK, Jacob Jansz, fl. 1643. (13)
URBINO (Urbini), Carlo, fl. c. 1550–8. (217–220)

ALCK, Adriaan, b. 1622. (13)
ALCKX, Pieter, 1734–85. (61)
AN DER PLANCKE, Jan, fl. 1715. (55)
AN DER VOORT, Michiel I, 1667–1737. (57)
AN DER WAGT, Dirk, fl. 1732. (28)
ERBECKT, Jacques, fl. 1747. (148)
ERBRUGGHEN, Pieter I, 1615–86. (51)
ERGAELEN, Jan, fl. 1667–9. (52)
ERHAEGEN, Theodor, 1701–59. (61)
GARNY, Felipe, d. 1543. (177)
AGENAAR, Jasper, fl. 1692. (20, 21)
ALWIJN, Emmanuel, fl. 1760–5. (60)
ESTERMAN, Jurriaan, fl. 1719–30. (24, 26)
AVERY (Savery), Jan Baptist, 1697–1742. (29)

Woodcarvers, sculptors and cabinet-makers

LFONSIN, Antonio, fl. 1705–9. (185)
RAÚJO, Marceliano de, fl. 1737–8. (188, 189)
ABEL, Johann Baptist, fl. 1749–75. (104, 105)
ACHELIER, Nicolas, 1485–c. 1566. (124)
AURSCHEIT, Jan Pieter van, I, 1669–1728. (56)
ELY, Jacques, fl. 1542–51. (127)
ERTRAND, David, fl. c. 1710. (140)
HORRI, Louis, fl. 1611. (129)
OULLIN, Nicolaes, fl. 1628. (47)
OYÉ, —, fl. 1773. (152)
URGUET, —, fl. 1773. (152)
URON, Jean, fl. 1631. (133)
ABIROL, —, fl. 1773. (152)
ARBONELL, Antonio, fl. 1539–41. (167)
ESSY, —, fl. 1773. (152)
HEMIN, Sainctot, fl. c. 1530–55. (123)
HRISTIAN, Joseph, 1706–77. (92, 94)
LAUWAERT, Michiel, fl. 1717–19. (55)
ORNET, Pierre, fl. 1638–40. (132)
ORTES, Manuel, fl. 1806. (202)
AL PIAZ, Giovanni Battista, fl. 1713. (240)
EL PINO Y VELASCO, Antonio, fl. 1712–15. (186)
ESY, Jacques, fl. 1643–53. (48)
UERR, Johann Georg, 1723–79. (101)
UGOULON, Jules, fl. 1698–1714. (140)
LSHOECHT, Jan, 1711–81. (62)
ANTONI, Andrea, 1659–1734. (238)
AVRE, Pierre, fl. 1789. (157)
EICHTMAYER, Joseph Anton, 1696–1770. (101)
ICHON, Jacques-François, fl. 1758–9. (150)
ONTANES, Simon, fl. 1737–8. (188, 189)
OUBERT, Rolland, fl. 1542–51. (127)
RILLEUX, Pierre, fl. 1638–40. (132)
RUEHOLZ, Joachim, fl. 1737–50. (83–85)
UCHS, Hans, 1517–61. (71)
ALLETTI, Carlo Andrea, fl. 1516–18. (208)
ARCÍA SEAREZ, Bernabé, fl. c. 1715–22. (187)
IBBONS, Grinling, 1648–1721. (255)

GIOVANNI D'ALESSO D'ANTONIO (Nanni Unghero), 1490–1546. (210)
GUSMOND, Raymond, fl. 1628. (128)
HALWIJN, Emmanuel, fl. c. 1760. (60)
HEIGENMANN, Georg, fl. 1657–60. (231)
HERNANDEZ, Juan, fl. 1796. (198)
HOERMANN, Martin, 1688–1782. (92–94)
HOSTRI, Perris, fl. c. 1560. (169–171)
JANSZ, Jan, fl. 1686. (18)
JEGG, Johann Christian, d. 1789. (106)
KOOLS, Hendrik, fl. 1535–40. (44)
LAECHLANT, Jacob Dirckz II, fl. 1668–71. (16)
LANDUCCI, Sante, fl. 1615. (226)
LEBLANC, —, fl. 1758–9. (150)
LOGTEREN, Jan van, 1709–45. (29)
LÓPEZ, Germán, fl. c. 1757–62. (191)
MALIEU, Christiaan, d. 1645. (48)
MANZANO, Alonso, fl. 1689. (192, 193)
MARCOVALDI, Giacomo, fl. 1555–6. (215)
MARLET, Edmé, fl. 1743. (147)
MARNEUF, Antoine-André, 1796–1865. (158)
MARTEAU, —, fl. 1710. (140)
MEEGH, Jan, fl. 1668–71. (16)
MEIJER, Allart, fl. 1691–1702. (19, 22)
MENGELBERG, Wilhelm, 1837–1919. (6)
MONGE, Pierre, fl. 1611. (129)
MONTANO, Giovanni Battista, 1534–1621. (224)
MORÉJOT, Antoine, fl. 1611. (129)
MORETO (Moretto), Giovanni da, fl. 1527. (173)
MOSCA, Bernardino, 1665–1733? (242)
MULLER, Symon, fl. 1692. (20, 21)
NERGER, Christian, d. 1708. (116)
PAZOS, Domingo Rodriguez de, fl. 1712–35. (186)
PERIS, François, fl. 1628. (47)
PIANTAVIGNA, Bartolomeo, fl. 1536–7. (213)
PIERSOTTE, A., fl. 1853–61. (64)
PIETRO CASTELNUOVO, Giovanni di, fl. 1519–23. (209)
PIETTE, Antoine-Joseph and Jean, fl. c. 1715–36. (141)
PILLON (Pilon), Germain (III?), fl. 1647. (135)
PULVIER, Dominique, fl. c. 1673. (254)
PUTTERE, Pieter de, fl. 1643–9. (48)
RÉBILLÉ, Nicolas, fl. 1764. (150)
REINHARD, Johannes, fl. 1774–82. (103)
ROMAY, Miguel de, fl. 1705–9. (185)
ROMBOUTS, Walram, c. 1598–1668. (49)
ROQUER, Pedro, fl. 1862. (199)
SALVALIERRA, Mariano, fl. 1796. (198)
SANZ, Antonio, fl. 1791–4. (172)
SASSE, Johann, fl. 1681. (74)
SAUVAGE, Jacques, fl. 1643–53. (48, 50)
SCABRINI, Paolo, fl. 1706. (240)
SCHAEFFER, Franz Ignatius and Jörg, fl. 1774–82. (103)
SCHALKEN, Jan, fl. 1589. (45)
SCHILLIGER, Felix Joseph, 1743–98. (107)
SCHUT, Jan Albertsz, fl. 1692. (20, 21)
SCHYSLER, Georg, fl. 1618. (12)
SCUDELLINO, Andrea, fl. 1560. (216)

Bibliography

The literature on organs and their cases is very extensive. In addition books, articles and periodicals specifically devoted to organs in very European language, there are many references to them in guide-books to individual cathedrals and churches and in regional guides of storical and/or archaeological interest, such as those issued by the istorical Monuments Commission in Britain or the Verein für eschichte und Altertumskunde Westfalens in Germany.

However, in a book whose appeal is intended to be mainly visual it felt that no great purpose would be served by including a long and etailed bibliography. Accordingly the following titles are those only books which are likely to be helpful towards a general understanding the organ case and its history. The reader who seeks for more etailed information should consult R. Reuter's invaluable *Bibliographie der Orgel* published by the University of Munster in 1973.

ZEVEDO, C. de. *Baroque organ cases of Portugal*. Amsterdam: Knuf 1972

URGEMEISTER, L. *Der Orgelbauer in Schlesien*. Strassburg: Heitz 1925

LUTTON, C. and NILAND, A. *The British organ*. London: Batsford 1963

AEHNERT, U. *Die Orgeln Gottfried Silbermanns in Mitteldeutschland*. Leipzig: Koehler & Amelang 1963

UFOURCQ, N. *Esquisse d'une histoire de l'orgue en France du XIIIe au XVIIIe siècle* [etc.]. Paris: Larousse, Droz 1935.

UFOURCQ, N. *Le livre de l'orgue français, 1589–1789*. 2 vols. Paris: Picard 1969–71

LADE, E. *Der Orgelbauer Gottfried Silbermann* [etc.]. Leipzig 1926.

ORER, A. *Orgeln in Oesterreich*. Wien: Schroll, 1973

REGOIR, E. G. J. *Historique de la facture et des facteurs d'orgue, avec la nomenclature des principales orgues placées dans les Pays-Bas et dans les provinces flamandes de la Belgique* [etc.]. (Facsimile of 1864 edn.). Amsterdam: Knuf 1972

Groningen: Stichting Groningen Orgelland. *Publicaties*, 1. 'Arp Schnitger, 1648–1719, en zijn werk in het Groningerland'. 1969

HILL, A. G. *The organ-cases and organs of the Middle Ages and Renaissance: a comprehensive essay* [etc.]. London: Bogue, 1883, 1891

HOPKINS, E. J. *The organ, its history and construction: a comprehensive treatise* [etc.]. [Reprint of 3rd edn., 1877.] Amsterdam: Knuf 1972

MUENGER, F. *Schweizer Orgeln von der Gotik bis zur Gegenwart*. Bern: Krompholz, 1973

Munster: University [Musikwissenschaftliches Seminar: Orgelwissenschaftliche Forschungsstelle]. *Veröffentlichungen*, 5. Fock, G. 'Arp Schnitger und seine Schule [etc.]'. 1974

NORBURY, J. *The box of whistles: an illustrated book on organ cases* [etc.]. London: Bradbury, Agnew & Co., 1877.

PEETERS, F. and VENTE, M. A. *The organ and its music in the Netherlands, 1500–1800*. Amsterdam: Mercatorfonds, 1971.

QUOIKA, R. *Ueber die Orgel in Altbayern* [etc.]. Berlin: Merseburger, 1968

SERVIÈRES, G. *La décoration artistique des buffets d'orgues*. Paris: van Oest, 1928

STUEVEN, W. *Orgel und Orgelbauer im halleschen Land vor 1800*. Wiesbaden: Breitkopf & Härtel, 1964

SUMNER, W. L. *The organ* [etc.]. 3rd edn. London: Macdonald, 1962

SUTTON, REV. F. H. *Church organs: their position and construction* [etc.]. 3rd edn. London: Rivingtons, 1883. [With the Appendix relating to the organ at Old Radnor]

VENTE, M. A. *Bouwstoffen tot de geschiedenis van het nederlandse orgel in de 16de eeuw* [etc.]. Amsterdam: H. Paris, 1942

VENTE, M. A. *Die Brabanter Orgel: zur Geschichte der Orgelkunst in Belgien und Holland im Zeitalter der Gotik und der Renaissance*. Amsterdam, 1958